A Guide
to
Public
Lending
Right

A Guide to Public Lending Right

Brigid Brophy

Gower　　**A Grafton Book**

*Published by
Gower Publishing Company Limited,
Gower House, Croft Road, Aldershot,
Hampshire GU11 3HR, England*

British Library Cataloguing in Publication Data

Brophy, Brigid
    A guide to public lending right
    1. Public lending rights (of author) — Great Britain
    I. Title
    344.104′92   KD1305.5

    ISBN 0–566–03485–9

Printed and bound in Great Britain by
Biddles Ltd, Guildford and King's Lynn

Contents

Preface

Part I is a basic anatomy of Public Lending Right. It is at the same time a comparative anatomy, which describes how (and, where discernible, why) one country's PLR system differs from another's.

Part II concentrates on PLR in Britain. It provides practical guidance for writers and illustrators, gives an account of the PLR administration, especially as that affects the libraries in the sample, and finishes with an outline of the PLR campaign.

I have received generous help from and am deeply grateful to: Giles Gordon; Walter J. Jeffrey; Mark Le Fanu; Shena Mackay; Charles Osborne; Jeremy Phillips; John Sumsion; Elizabeth Thomas; David Whitaker.

BRIGID BROPHY

Part I   The elements of PLR

1 Practice

1.1 What?

Public Lending Right (PLR) is the conspicuously non-self-explanatory name given in English-speaking countries to the entitlement of a creator to be paid for the use the public makes of his work by means of libraries.

The English and other names are discussed in 2.1.

1.2 When? Where?

By 1982 Public Lending Right systems were in operation in seven countries. They are, with the dates when they decided to institute PLR:

Denmark, 1946
Sweden, 1954, with extension in 1957 (see 1.8)
Iceland, 1963
Federal Republic of Germany (West Germany), 1972
New Zealand, 1973
Australia, 1974
Great Britain, 1979–82.

In Germany, the copyright statute (or, correctly, the creator's right – *Urheberrecht* – statute) of 1965 gave the creator of a copyright work the right to fair payment when his work was lent 'for the financial gain of the lender'. Since, however, most libraries in Germany were non-profit-making and many of them publicly funded, that provision could not be made the springboard for a practical PLR system. In 1972, the Article (no. 27 of the statute) was extended to cover all libraries accessible to the public, and it was therefore in 1972 that Germany took the effective decision to institute PLR.

Between the decision to institute it and the first PLR payments there was, in most countries, a pause, usually of a year or two, because an administrative apparatus had meanwhile to be set up to calculate and distribute the payments, which are in all cases made once a year. In some countries, the first round of payments was backdated to the time of the decision.

1

In Britain (where there was no backdating), the pause was uniquely long, because PLR was, uniquely, introduced by a two-leg process. The author's right to payment was created by an Act of Parliament passed in March 1979 (the Public Lending Right Act, 1979). The Act itself, however, required secondary legislation to be drafted to set out the details of the PLR system. That was not done until three years after the passage of the Act. The secondary legislation (the Public Lending Right Scheme, 1982) received parliamentary approval in April 1982. Only after that, in September 1982, could the administration of PLR be activated, and it was announced that the first payments were due in February 1984.

Apart from their unanimous recognition that it is administratively convenient to make payments once a year, requiting the creator for a year's library use of his work during the preceding period, the seven functioning PLR systems are extremely diverse. The systems in New Zealand and Australia resemble one another but are not identical. Indeed, there is not a PLR system in operation that is identical in all aspects or even in several major aspects with any other system.

1.3 On what?

Books are what lending libraries were invented to lend, and books remain the overwhelmingly major subject of their activities.

In Britain and elsewhere, libraries began in the 20th century to lend gramophone records, and in some cases works of visual art, as well as books. Even so, when PLR legislation was introduced in Britain in the 1970s, objects other than books accounted for only about one per cent of all loans made from public libraries. According to CIPFA (Chartered Institute of Public Finance and Accountancy) figures (see further 5.11), by the year 1980–81 loans of records, cassettes and tapes still represented only two per cent of all public-library loans.

Realistically tackling the largest part of the problem, six of the seven countries that recognise PLR recognise it only in relation to books.

The Federal Republic of Germany is the only country to have instituted PLR under copyright (or, as it is in Germany, creator's right) law. Having done so, it was in self-consistency bound to recognise PLR in all works in which copyright subsists, namely literary, dramatic, musical and visual-arts works. Even in Germany, however, books (or, to be exact, printed words) absorb by far the largest portion of the funds allocated to PLR.

The statute under which German PLR operates insists that the creator's claim to PLR can be exercised only through a collecting society, that is, a copyright-utilisation society for the collective exercise of rights individually held under copyright. A collecting society is not a government agency but an organisation formed by or on behalf of the creators of copyright works. The administration of PLR in Germany is divided between three collecting societies which deal, respectively, with literature, music and the visual arts (including photography).

The three German collecting societies jointly negotiate the sum that is annually allocated to PLR by the Federal (central) and Länder (regional) governments. (The sum can be re-negotiated every two years.) The collecting societies then negotiate between themselves the apportionment of the allocation.

The collecting society VG (Verwertungsgesellschaft) WORT, which, as its name implies, administers PLR on words (that is, in practice, on books and on pieces of journalism of three pages' length and above) takes, to cite the portion for 1982, 91.2 per cent of the total sum allocated to PLR.

In Britain, the first PLR Bill to be introduced by a government proposed to recognise PLR in books alone. The campaign to persuade the government to introduce legislation had been conducted by writers of books, and notably by Writers Action Group (WAG), and writers expected their profession to be the major beneficiaries. They were, however, anxious to secure a fair share of PLR for creators of other kinds, and an amendment to the Bill was moved in the House of Lords by Lord Willis (Ted Willis, the novelist and dramatist, an active member both of WAG and of the Writers' Guild of Great Britain) to change the word 'books' in the appropriate parts of the Bill to 'works', with the intention of making PLR payable on all objects, books and other-than-books, lent from the libraries. The amendment was not, however, acceptable to the government.

That first government PLR Bill in Britain was introduced by a Labour government with the front-bench support of all parties. On the back benches of the House of Commons, however, it encountered a two-party (Conservative and Labour) filibuster conducted by eight Members. Though not defeated, the Bill ran out or, rather, was filibustered out of parliamentary time at the end of the parliamentary Session in November 1976. It was a second Bill, in all essentials the same and again introduced by the Labour government with all-party support, that was eventually passed and became the Public Lending Right Act of 1979.

Under that Act, PLR in Britain is confined to books. And as a matter of fact there was a sound technical reason for the government's decision that it should be so.

1.4 Titles and ISBNs

In any PLR system where, as in Britain, the author's payment is proportionate to the number of loans made of his work, the chief technical problem consists in identifying the titles concerned in order to keep count of the number of loans of each.

The word 'title' is here used in its book-trade sense, where it means not the literal title but the literary work that goes under that title.

All discussions of books are prone to confusion unless they distinguish, where the context demands, between the title, which is the literary work created by the author, and the copies of it that are printed by the printer, sold by booksellers and lent by libraries.

The exceptional confusion shown during the PLR debates in Parliament was partly caused by the failure of the legislation to make it clear when it was speaking of a title and when of a copy (or a volume). The PLR Act of 1979 uses the word 'book' in both senses indiscriminately. It defines libraries as 'collections of books', where it might more happily have used the word 'volumes'; and it requires the Registrar of PLR to keep a register showing 'the books in respect of which Public Lending Right subsists' when what the Registrar in fact keeps is a list not of the copies or volumes in libraries but of the titles eligible for PLR.

So long as PLR is paid only on literary works, it is not too difficult, even given the unique size of the library network in Britain (see further 2.4), to link the copies that are lent from the libraries to the title that thereby earns PLR. That is because a system of unique numbering already exists, in the form of the ISBN (International Standard Book Number).

The ISBN consists of a ten-digit code number, which the publisher causes to be printed in the volume. Each ISBN is unique to, and can therefore be used to identify, a particular title in a particular edition. That is to say, different editions (for instance, the hardback and the paperback) of the same title have different ISBNs.

ISBNs were introduced in Britain in 1968. Since then, British publishers have increasingly taken to having the appropriate ISBN printed in every copy of every title they publish, because the ISBN makes it possible for copies to be ordered, distributed and documented by automatic processes.

Adopted by publishers for their own purposes, ISBNs, by sparing the PLR administration the expense of imposing its own equivalent, have become cardinal to the practical and cheap operation of PLR in Britain.

When the PLR administration began functioning in 1982–3, libraries still contained volumes printed before the ISBN came into widespread use. Even as early as 1976, however, some 68 per cent of the lending volumes in public libraries already had ISBNs printed in them, and the proportion naturally increases as pre-ISBN volumes are discarded from libraries and replaced by new publications (or by new reprints of old publications) carrying the ISBN.

As a working operation, PLR in Britain consists of collecting and comparing two sets of information: a record, supplied by libraries, of the volumes that have been lent; and a list (the register), supplied by the applications of authors, of titles eligible to earn PLR. By comparing one set of data with the other, the PLR administration calculates the number of loans made of each title and thus the amount of payment the title has earned.

Thanks to the ISBN, all these processes can be conducted by automated methods. The list of eligible titles is held on computer together with the ISBN of each (or, when there is more than one edition of the title, the ISBNs). Even where a title does not possess an ISBN, the nature of the code (which is further described in 5.8) is such that the PLR administration can allocate it a 'pseudo-ISBN' within the idiom of the code that will not be duplicated by any real, existing ISBN.

For the libraries, given that a high proportion of the volumes lent have ISBNs printed in them, it is not difficult to

5

record loans in terms of ISBNs (which the PLR administration supplements, where necessary, in its own files by 'pseudo-ISBNs'). Alternatively, if libraries prefer to record loans by internal numbering systems of their own, such as the accession numbers of the volumes in the collection, the ISBN provides a universal language into which the PLR administration can translate records kept under various incompatible numbering systems before matching them with the register of ISBNs eligible to earn PLR.

1.5 The books-only decision in Britain

In 1974–5, when the British government tested the plan for computerised PLR put forward by Writers Action Group, it was clear that the ISBN had already penetrated deeply enough into the libraries to serve as the basic identifying code of a computerised PLR system dealing with books.

The hope of Writers Action Group that the system would deal also with gramophone records and cassettes was frustrated by the fact that no equivalent to the ISBN was to hand for identifying which titles had been lent. In the area of records and cassettes there was no universal system of unique numbering.

It would be possible to devise such a system and mark the appropriate numbers bodily on the objects available for loan, but it would be costly and, moreover, disproportionately costly. The administrative cost of paying PLR on a gramophone record would be higher than that of paying it on a volume. Thus the proportionately highest administration costs would be spent on the articles that accounted for the smallest part of library activity (cf. 1.3).

This was a telling consideration because, from the moment that the British government seriously considered introducing PLR, it insisted that it would allocate a total sum to PLR, from which the administration costs must be paid first, only the remainder then being divided among the creators in proportion to the loans of each creator's work. To include gramophone records and cassettes in the PLR system would have meant either allocating them their own small proportion of the PLR total, which would have been swallowed up by their high administration costs, or taking their costs out of the main pool, thus seriously reducing the payment per loan to all creators, the majority of whom were creators of books.

In those circumstances the government's decision was inevitably that PLR in Britain should be paid only on books.

1.6 On what basis?

There are two (mutually exclusive) bases on which a PLR system can calculate the amount of PLR earned by each title. The seven PLR systems in operation are roughly evenly divided between the two. Either

1 payment is proportionate to the number of copies of the title in question that was present in the libraries' stocks during the period that is being paid for (the stock-census or shelf-fee method)

or

2 payment is proportionate to the total number of loans made, during the year that is being paid for, of the title in question (the loans-based method).

Method 1 pays the author for the availability of the title in the libraries. The amount the author receives does not vary in reflection of whether the public chooses to take advantage of that availability or, if it does, to what extent. The same sum is earned by a volume that spends the year untouched on the library shelf as by a volume that is borrowed 20 times.

Indeed, there is even a danger that the authors whose works are in the smallest demand with the public will in the long run collect the most PLR, since seldom-borrowed volumes are likely to last longer than much-borrowed volumes and thus survive to earn their shelf-fee time after time. In practice, however, there are unlikely to be many copies in libraries of titles that are in small demand, and two of the countries that pay a shelf-fee, New Zealand and Australia, make no payment unless there are at least 50 copies of the title in the libraries.

Even so, one of the dangers inherent in the shelf-fee method is visible in the rule by which the New Zealand PLR system guards against it: no fee is paid on a volume donated to a library unless the chief librarian certifies that the library would have bought a copy of that title had one not been donated.

The shelf-fee or stock-census method operates in Denmark, Iceland, New Zealand and Australia, all of which have small populations and, in relation to population, small or no more than medium-sized library networks.

Technically, the stock-census method consists of matching a list of eligible titles, whose authors have applied for PLR on them, to a census, provided by the libraries, of the titles (plus the number of copies held of each) to be found in the library stock or in the library catalogues.

In Denmark and in Iceland (in the latter of which the libraries are required to make a return of the number of copies they hold of each title before 1 October in each year), payment is calculated on the basis of a comprehensive annual census of library stocks. In New Zealand a survey of titles in stock takes place approximately every five years, though it is updated in the interim with new titles published in the meantime. It consists of a full survey of large libraries, with an estimate, from a random sample, of the stocks held by smaller libraries. Australia operates what is in effect a sample census over a three-year cycle. The list of titles on which PLR can legitimately be claimed is divided into three portions, one of which is sent each year to a statistically selected sample of libraries, which record how many copies they hold of each title listed.

Method 2, by which payment is proportionate to the number of loans of each title, is operated in Sweden, in Great Britain and, on 'belletristic' (that is, general as distinct from specialist scientific) books, by VG WORT, the collecting society that administers PLR on literary works in Germany (cf. 1.3).

Two of these countries (Sweden and Britain) have exceptionally large library networks. If size is judged by the number of loans made annually, the Swedish library system is unusually large in relation to population. Judged by the same standard, the library system in Britain is the largest in the western world, not only in relation to population but in absolute terms.

All the loans-based systems assess the total number of loans made of each title from a sample of loans. They are all, in fact, loans-sampling systems. Payment is calculated by comparing the list of titles eligible to earn PLR with the loans records supplied by (or, in the case of VG WORT, taken from) a sample of libraries, to determine how many loans each eligible title has chalked up in the sample of loans.

To pay PLR on the basis of loans is in effect to pay the author for the borrower's decision to take the book out of the library. By contrast, the stock-census method, which pays according to the availability of the title on the shelf, is in effect paying the author for the library's decision to buy a copy of the title and keep it in the library stock. Under the stock-census method, a volume, once bought by a library, earns PLR whether or not anyone borrows it. Under the loans-based method, a volume placed on the library shelf does not earn PLR unless a borrower decides to take it out. Under the stock-census method it is librarians, under the loans-based method the borrowers, who determine how much PLR an author earns.

In Britain, fundamentalist objectors to PLR sometimes go so far as to complain that the PLR payment reflects the borrower's decision to take the book home instead of his consumer-satisfaction with it when he gets it home. The borrower's decision to borrow the book is recorded when the book is checked out of the library. Complainants have not suggested a method that could record, let alone record accurately, the reader's satisfaction or dissatisfaction. And as a matter of fact even a book that dissatisfies him may do its reader a service, even if only by helping him define his own taste. The quaint complaint that loans-based PLR systems pay for the decision to borrow a book rather than pleasure taken in the book borrowed ignores the fact that borrowers have unrestricted opportunity to examine the works on offer before making their choice, an opportunity not given to buyers of theatre tickets or users of the public health or education services, and seems to be less an objection than a flight of rhetoric against PLR.

This complaint against loans-based PLR is often uttered in the same breath or paragraph as a second complaint that is scarcely compatible with the first. In the first complaint, the borrower chooses the book but may not enjoy it, in which case, according to the complaint, the author should not be paid. In the second complaint, the borrower may enjoy the book but the author should not be paid if the complainant would not have enjoyed it or thinks that the borrower ought not to have done: if, that is to say, the book is what the complainant judges to be a 'bad' book. One of the disquieting disclosures of the PLR debates in the House of Commons was the number of MPs who assumed that the difference between a good and a bad work of literature can be told as readily and as infallibly as the difference between a mauve binding and a green one. Many suggestions were made that PLR should be paid only on 'good' books, but no firm suggestion was offered about who should perform the act of aesthetic judgement, how, given the huge number of titles to be judged, the judges should be paid or what should be done when, as happens weekly on the review pages of the papers, there was a conflict between informed opinions.

The writers' answers to these rhetorical attempts to discredit PLR were: there may be such things as absolute aesthetic standards, but there are no proveably and demonstrably absolute aesthetic standards; and the person best placed to judge what is for him a good book is the person who chooses to borrow it. It is a fallacy entertained only by people not conversant with literature that supreme writers can be encouraged to exist in isolation. This usually accompanies the fallacy that someone exists who can recognise a supreme writer at a glance. As a rule, literature comes into being in busy and excited literary climates. Supremacists should study the work of the contemporaries of Shakespeare and remember how little evidence there is that he was universally recognised as supreme at the time. It can be argued that public funds can best serve literature by methods which, like a generously-funded loans-based PLR, keep the entire (and indispensable) literary climate alive.

1.7 Loans sampling

In a library network of any size, the cost of collecting and processing for PLR all the records of all the loans made from all the libraries would be prohibitive. In Britain, where administrative costs are taken out of the PLR fund first, that would leave nothing or virtually nothing for making payments to the authors.

Loans-based systems therefore assess the total number of each title's loans from a sample of loans. In Britain, the sample returns are 'grossed up', area by area, in proportion to the totality of library loans. For stock-census systems, sampling is an option, which is taken in New Zealand and Australia (cf. 1.6). For loans-based systems, it is an economic necessity.

The British PLR Act of 1979, whatever else it may be careless about (cf. 1.4), takes care to make the author's entitlement to PLR depend not on the total number of loans made of his work but on the number of loans made of it by the libraries in the sample. That precaution was needed in order to spare the PLR administration and, ultimately, the government from the claims (correct, deluded or simply unverifiable) of authors who might believe or suspect their work to have been lent more often than appeared from the sample.

Understandably, however, many MPs failed during the PLR debates to recognise that, when the PLR Bill (eventually the PLR Act of 1979) provided for entitlement to PLR to depend on 'the number of occasions on which books are lent out from particular libraries', what it meant by the 'particular libraries' were the libraries in a carefully sited sample. The word 'sampling' entered the legislation only with the PLR Scheme of 1982 (cf. 1.2).

Sampling methods vary in the accuracy they attain, and PLR systems vary in the accuracy their samples need to try to attain. In Britain, the idea of sampling was suggested by Writers Action Group, and sceptical governments laid down rigorous conditions and tested the proposed sample exhaustively. In Germany, the administration of PLR is entrusted by statute to collecting societies that administer the rights of the creators of the works on which PLR is paid (cf. 1.3 and 1.6). In Germany it is, therefore, chiefly the creators themselves who have to be satisfied by the administration of PLR, though (under a separate statute) the collecting societies are subject to supervision by the German patents office.

In relation to the majority of the authors whose PLR it administers (see further 2.7), VG WORT, the German collecting society that deals with books and journalism, operates a spot-check on loans, in which loans are recorded by photographing the title-pages of the works lent. The spot-check takes place during two three-week periods (spring and autumn), in selected libraries in seven towns, once a year. The results of each year's spot-check are melded with the results of the spot-checks of the previous two years.

The Swedish sample is more, and the British sample very much more, widely-based.

In Britain, the sample consists of the entire loans records, for the whole of a year, from each of 16 libraries. From the moment that sampling began (1 January 1983), the system provided for a complete sample of libraries to be always in existence, taking the loans record continuously.

The 16 sample libraries are diverse in size and character and are dispersed throughout the United Kingdom in such a way that the sample constitutes a representative model, geographically and socially, of the national library network.

The accuracy of the sample is further improved by 'rotation', which increases the likelihood that accidental distortions will be cancelled out over a course of years. In Britain the sample is 'rotated' by dropping all 16 libraries from the sample every four years (at the rate of four libraries dropped a year) and replacing them by fresh libraries in the statistically appropriate areas and of the statistically appropriate character.

The accuracy of a sample increases when its size (relative to the whole) increases, but so does its cost. By 1983, when the first loans sample began to be taken in Britain, it was possible to obtain a highly accurate but not enormous sample at comparatively low cost, thanks to the advance of automation in the library network. Where a library, for its own purposes, keeps a computer record of its loans, the PLR administration can, comparatively cheaply and easily (though it may have to convert or translate the data), use that record as part of the PLR sample. So many libraries are now computerised that, in almost every area and category nominated by the statistical pattern of the sample, it is possible for the PLR administration to minimise costs by choosing for the sample a library that is computerised and even to replace that library by another computerised library in the course of 'rotation'.

The British sample is also, however, a feat of statistical ingenuity. When Writers Action Group encountered government and civil service scepticism about its proposal of a sample, it sought and was generously given the advice of a statistician (Mr R. A. Pluck) and of a firm of computer consultants (Logica). When, thanks to their demonstrations and mathematical models, the government was eventually convinced that cheap and accurate sampling was feasible, it sensibly took over the experts who had advised Writers Action Group, and it was largely they who, having pioneered the matter in Britain, designed the British sample and the technical operation of the British PLR system.

1.8 Volumes kept in libraries

As a method of measuring and paying for the use the public chooses to make of a given title, a loans-based PLR system is obviously more accurate than the type of system that pays for the presence of the title in the library stock or catalogue irrespective of whether copies of that title are ever borrowed or not (cf. 1.6).

The shelf-fee has only one advantage over the loans payment: it automatically deals, though it does not deal accurately, with volumes that are kept on library premises and are not allowed to be taken home by a borrower.

These volumes are kept in reference libraries or in the reference sections of lending libraries and are consulted by the public on library premises. A PLR system that is based on a stock-census includes such volumes in its census. A loans-based system cannot in itself deal with them (though it can add a method of dealing with them), because what it records are 'loans across the counter' and it does not take into account volumes that are not permitted to cross the counter.

In British public libraries, whether a volume is classified as lending stock or reference stock is a decision made by the individual library. There are titles that are classified as lending stock in one library and reference stock in another.

This one merit of the stock-census method does not, however, outweigh its demerits in failing to reflect the amount of use the public makes of any volume, of whatever kind. The accuracy with which loans-based systems record the use made of lending volumes must count as the greater merit, because lending volumes greatly outnumber reference volumes.

In public libraries in Britain, according to figures worked out in 1974–5, reference volumes constitute only 12 per cent of the total library stock. In making payment on the loans of lending volumes the British PLR system can claim to be dealing, and dealing accurately, with 88 per cent of the problem.

That does not, however, argue that it is fair simply to deprive the authors of the reference volumes of any entitlement to PLR. No payment on volumes retained in reference libraries or sections is made by the British PLR system or by the PLR system administered in Germany by VG WORT (cf. 1.3, 1.6 and 1.7).

The ideal method of calculating payments on reference volumes is by means of a sample of actual consultations on library premises. Librarians everywhere, however, consider that the taking of such a sample would grossly disrupt the routine of the library (an objection that cannot be made to the sampling of loans, since checking volumes in and out across the library counter is part of the library routine because the library must keep track of its volumes).

Accordingly, the Swedish PLR system has devised an admittedly second-best method of calculating payments on volumes held in reference libraries and sections. This consists in essence of paying an annual shelf-fee (cf. 1.6) on titles that show up in a census (taken, in Sweden, not annually but in certain years) of titles in reference stock. The fee paid per year on a reference volume is equal to the sum earned by a lending volume that has been borrowed the average number of times in a year.

PLR in Sweden was initiated with loans payments on lending volumes. The decision to make payments also on volumes held as reference stock was taken three years later, in 1957. The two systems of calculating payment operate separately but in parallel, and some authors of diverse types of title receive payments under both systems.

In Britain, while Writers Action Group was urging the government to introduce PLR legislation, it urged that Britain should adopt the Swedish double system of calculating payments. A 'Technical Investigation Group' set up by the minister for the arts in 1974 established that it would be feasible and not forbiddingly expensive to take annually a representative sample census of titles in reference stocks, which could be the basis for calculating annual reference payments. The PLR legislation, however, when it was eventually introduced, proved to make no provision for payment on reference stock.

It appeared that the government's objection to the payment on reference stock was that the sum paid per volume would be 'arbitrary'. So, indeed, it would be, in comparison with the very precisely related-to-use payments on loans, though not in comparison with any payment in any stock-census system. However, to ignore the claim to PLR of the authors of reference volumes is even more arbitrary. Those authors would prefer an 'arbitrary' payment to none. Neither need the authors of lending volumes have felt robbed if the common PLR fund were to make payments on reference volumes based on the average PLR earnings of lending volumes, since the fee, while no doubt over-generous to some reference volumes, would probably also be under-generous to others.

The cause of the reference stock continued, in 1983, to be pressed (see 4.3) by the two trade unions of writers, the Writers' Guild of Great Britain and the Society of Authors. (Writers

Action Group dissolved in 1982, having achieved its main objective of loans payments on lending volumes.) British authors may take heart from the Swedish demonstration that a PLR system that begins with payments on loans of lending volumes may later add reference payments.

1.9 Which libraries?

PLR systems pay for the use (when the system is loans-based) or the presence (when it is stock-census-based) of titles in libraries. To the crucial question 'Which libraries?', however, the various national systems return various answers, dependent partly on administrative (and sometimes legislative) convenience but also in reflection of diverse opinions about what the taxpayer, who is the ultimate source of PLR funds, can justifiably be asked to pay for.

In Sweden both the loans sample and the stock-census of reference volumes (cf. 1.8) are taken from public libraries only, with the result that it is only public-library use of books that is being paid for. In Britain the loans sample (cf. 1.7) is taken from public libraries only and its results are grossed up to represent the totality of loans from public libraries only.

By contrast, the spot-check on loans conducted by VG WORT in Germany (cf. 1.7) samples public, university, prison and church libraries and also libraries run by firms for the use of their employees, although all the funding of PLR is derived from government sources.

The stock-census in Denmark comprehends public and school libraries, that in Iceland public libraries only. In Australia the stock-census deals with public libraries only. In New Zealand it deals with titles in public, university and teachers' college libraries and also with titles in the Country Library and School Library services.

In Britain the term 'public library' has a highly specific meaning, not always understood in its full sense elsewhere. The public-library network dates from an Act of 1850 that permitted local authorities to spend part of their revenue from the rates on providing libraries that should lend books without charge to the borrower. The network was regularised and brought under the Department of Education and Science by the Public Libraries and Museums Act of 1964, which positively requires the local authorities 'to provide a comprehensive and

15

efficient library service for all persons' in the district 'desiring to make use thereof' (section 7, 1) and which forbids them (section 8, 1, 2 and 3) to charge for the lending of books, though it permits them to charge for the lending of articles other than books and to charge notification fees and fines on books.

In practice, the public libraries are funded partly at local level by rates and partly from central funds at national level by means of the rate support grant, which is disbursed to local authorities by the Department of the Environment.

In terms of the number of loans made, the public libraries are almost certainly the largest sector of the lending industry in Britain. (Not all the other types of library issue figures for the loans made.) By dealing with loans from the public libraries the British PLR system can again claim to be dealing with the major part of the problem.

It is not, however, the only substantial part of the problem. Lending takes place, in some instances in considerable quantity, from university, college, school and institutional libraries and even from sporadic survivals or revivals of the commercial libraries that were ubiquitous in the 19th century and early in the 20th.

On loans made from all those libraries that do not come within the technical meaning of 'public library' no PLR is paid.

It was inevitable that a PLR system in Britain should at least begin by tackling the public libraries, both because of the size of the network and because its nature makes it an easy place for a new administrative apparatus to start. The public libraries are in essentials, though not in minor matters, uniform; they are interlocking; and local and central data about their activities are easy to come by.

Moreover, since the Public Libraries and Museums Act of 1964 had already brought them within the purview of Parliament and under the direction of the Department of Education and Science, it must have seemed legislatively easy for the Public Lending Right Act of 1979 to require them to provide the loans sample and other data necessary to operating PLR.

In addition, it can be argued with some force that it is only the public libraries that are deliberately maintained as a national-plus-local institution, indeed a form of public service, by the will of Parliament and people, and from that it may seem to follow that only when it is through the public libraries that the public makes use of an author's work that Parliament can properly require the author to be paid his PLR by the taxpayer.

Indeed, it can justly be said that, if a boy at a privately-owned preparatory school takes a book out of his school library or if a member of a social club takes one out of the club's library, then it is the proprietors of the prep school and the club who are profiting by the author's work and that it is from them, not the taxpayer, that the author should seek his PLR.

The author has, however, no means of doing so. Parliament has legislated into being an apparatus to administer PLR and a fund to pay for it that function exclusively in relation to the public libraries. It has not given the author any statutory right, let alone any practical means of exercising it, to PLR in relation to the other-than-public libraries.

In Germany, where the author has such a right under copyright law (cf. 1.3), it is notable that it does not save the taxpayer any money. It is business firms and churches that benefit from running libraries for the entertainment or instruction of their employees or congregations, but, although technically the claim that VG WORT exerts on behalf of the authors is on the libraries themselves, the PLR that VG WORT distributes to authors whose books are lent from such libraries is provided, through government channels, by the taxpayer.

As a matter of fact, a claim under copyright on a multiplicity of institutions is of no use whatever to the individual copyright-owner unless the legislation that confers it also provides for its practical, which means in effect its collective, exercise. In Britain the owners of musical copyrights can enforce their claim to performing right only through a collecting society, the Performing Right Society, whose existence is statutorily acknowledged. In Germany the claim under copyright to PLR can by statute be exercised only through a recognised collecting society, though the statute does not limit the number of collecting societies that might be formed and win recognition.

To be effective, PLR legislation in any country must not only give a right but establish an organisation (or, as in Germany, provide for others to establish organisations) through which alone the right can be exercised. All PLR legislation everywhere is directed to avoiding the anarchy that would result if each individual author had the right and in practice the need to approach each individual library demanding an account of, and payment for, the loans that that library had made of his work.

In Britain the PLR Act of 1979 takes such measures by establishing a system of registration. Only by applying for and gaining registration can an author exercise the right to payment on his library loans which the Act confers on him. However, the payment a registered author can earn is payment on loans only from public libraries. In relation to loans from all the libraries of other types the PLR Act of 1979 left British authors exactly where they were before, namely unpaid.

To make British authors entitled to payment on all library loans, amending (or fresh) legislation would be needed.

British authors cannot, however, seek the rights denied them under the PLR Act of 1979 by means of an amendment to the Copyright Act of 1956.

Such a solution was feasible in Germany, but only because *Urheberrecht*, though often translated 'copyright', differs crucially from British copyright.

The German statute of 1965 vests the right invariably in the creator of the work and makes it inalienable from him during his lifetime (Articles 7 and 29). By contrast, the British Copyright Act of 1956 does not invariably make the creator of the work the owner of the copyright in it even to begin with; and even when he is the first owner he is highly vulnerable to being dispossessed of his copyright during his lifetime.

So long as British copyright law remains unreformed in this respect (a subject further discussed in the PLR context in 2.1), it is not an apt vehicle for Parliament to use in conferring rights on creators. It can confer rights only on copyright-owners, some of whom are and some of whom are not the creators of the work in which the copyright subsists.

For this reason, PLR legislation in Britain was not undertaken under copyright law but through an independent statute that specifically conferred the right on authors.

For the same reason, it is not (in the absence of major reform) to copyright law but to the PLR Act of 1979 that British authors must seek an extension (see further 4.3) to confer PLR on them in relation to loans made from other-than-public libraries.

1.10 Whose authors? And anyone else?

On the question whether they restrict their PLR payments to authors of a particular nationality or country of residence, PLR systems return less divergent answers than they do on many important questions. Indeed, six out of the seven systems in operation agree in requiring some qualification of nationality or residence to be met before they will recognise an author as eligible to be paid PLR.

In the answers to this question it is possible to glimpse, though not systematically to discern, some of the secondary functions which a PLR system may be expected to perform.

The Danish, Swedish and Icelandic systems make payment only to authors of, respectively, Danish, Swedish and Icelandic nationality.

In all three cases, the PLR system is directed to giving support exclusively to a native language and a native literary tradition that are vulnerable to encroachment from outside because the population to which they are native is comparatively small.

In a similar way, the PLR systems of New Zealand and Australia are designed to defend not only the local literary tradition but also the local variety of the English language against the numerically more powerful varieties spoken and written in Britain and the USA.

PLR in New Zealand is paid exclusively to (a) authors who are New Zealand citizens and who are also permanently resident in New Zealand and (b) authors who are not citizens of but are permanently resident in New Zealand, though in this case payment is made only on titles published since the author became a resident of New Zealand.

Australian PLR is paid exclusively to (a) authors who are Australian citizens, no matter where resident, and (b) authors, of no matter what nationality, who are normally resident in Australia, payment being made in this case irrespective of where the title in question was published.

The Australian PLR system seems also to be defending a local publishing industry against the more powerful British and the much more powerful US publishing industries, since payment is made not only to authors but (at a rate equivalent to 25 per cent of the fee paid to the author on each copy shewn in the sample stock-census) to publishers, provided that the publisher's business is carried on in Australia.

The Australian PLR system and the system administered in Germany by VG WORT (cf. 1.3 and 1.6–1.8) are the only systems that make payment to publishers as well as authors.

The rules of the British PLR system include a nationality-plus-residence qualification that indicates a need to defend a PLR fund that is exiguous in comparison with the (unmatched) size of the library network, while at the same time avoiding violation of the obligations of EEC membership.

Under the rules laid down by the government in the PLR Scheme of 1982 (cf. 1.2), British PLR is paid only to authors who are both (a) citizens of Britain or of some other member state of the EEC (European Economic Community) and (b) resident in the United Kingdom.

Most of the volumes borrowed from public libraries in Britain are in the English language. A small but noticeable portion of these are by North American authors and a smaller portion by Australasian authors. When in the course of campaigning for PLR in Britain Writers Action Group learned how tiny a sum the government was proposing to allocate to PLR (originally £1 million a year, later raised to £2 million), it was concerned to prevent the fund from being drained by payments to overseas countries from which no PLR payments could flow in return to British authors. Because of the common language, the chief threats to the fund were North America and Australasia. From North America no PLR could reach British authors in return, because neither Canada nor the USA has instituted PLR. From Australasia, equally, there could be no hope of PLR for British authors, since the systems of both New Zealand and Australia make payment only to their own nationals. The campaign sought, however, to make British PLR payable to authors in any overseas country that paid or should in future pay PLR to British authors.

The nationality-plus-residence requirement which the British government in the event introduced quiets the campaigners' major fear, in that it does prevent the tiny fund from being drained off to the large English-speaking countries from which no PLR can be expected by British authors in return, but the requirement was not, in the PLR Scheme of 1982, modified by any provision for reciprocity with countries that are prepared to pay PLR to British authors.

The British government could not have introduced a Britons-only PLR system without risking contravening Article 7 of the Treaty of Rome, which forbids discrimination between one EEC citizen and another on grounds of nationality. It is true that Denmark manages to belong to the EEC and to operate a Danes-only PLR system, but Denmark is better placed to resist reproach than Britain would have been had it introduced PLR for its own nationals only, because the Danish PLR system, with its Danes-only rule, had been operating since before the EEC was formed, whereas Britain joined the Community before instituting PLR.

However, by combining a nationality rule that opens British PLR to all citizens of EEC member states with a residence rule that restricts it to residents of the United Kingdom, the British PLR system achieves virtually the same effect as it would have done by a Britons-only rule, since the number of EEC authors residing in Britain can be relied on to be negligible. Why a nationality rule was thought necessary is unknown. A residence rule on its own would prevent payments to EEC and other countries that pay no PLR to British authors. authors.

Such EEC countries are the majority. Indeed, only three EEC member states (Denmark, West Germany and Britain) operate PLR at all. Of those three, only Germany does so without (at least formally) imposing restrictions according to nationality or residence.

The nationality-plus-residence rule in the British PLR system produces anomalies. A British author resident in Luxembourg is not eligible for British PLR; a Luxembourgeois author resident in Britain is. In many cases, the anomalies fell with ironic harshness on the campaigners for PLR. Some of the most generous contributors to the funds of Writers Action Group were British authors living abroad, who, when the nationality-plus-residence requirement was published in 1982, found themselves excluded, on grounds of residence, from the PLR their contributions had helped to win. Others, who not only contributed to but marched and lobbied with Writers Action Group, found themselves, though qualified by residence, disqualified by possessing a non-EEC nationality.

The only PLR systems to make (nominally at least) no conditions about nationality or residence are those operated by the collecting societies in West Germany. This follows consistently from the German decision to institute PLR under creator's right or copyright law (cf. 1.3), which is subject to the international copyright conventions (that is, the Berne and the Universal Copyright Conventions).

In practice, however, restrictions are, in a patchy way, imposed by the statutory provision in Germany that the right can be exercised only through a collecting society. Only German and German-resident non-German authors are eligible to have their PLR administered by VG WORT, the major PLR agency, a limitation that was still in operation in 1982, though a distant possibility had been by then glimpsed that European law might enforce a change. In effect, therefore, a non-German author who does not live in Germany can be paid his German PLR only if (a) there is a literary collecting society in his own country, (b) he joins it and (c) it can make an agreement with VG WORT under which VG WORT passes the PLR earned by his books in German libraries to his collecting society, which passes it to him. The PLR payment that VG WORT makes to publishers is made only to German publishers.

In addition, VG WORT, like other German collecting societies, does not pay the whole sum he earns in PLR to the author concerned but puts 55 per cent of it into communal funds for the collective benefit of authors. (This is further discussed in 2.5.) Authors who are not German are not allowed to benefit from the communal funds.

1.11 The ALCS

In Britain, the Authors' Lending and Copyright Society, Limited (ALCS), a literary collecting society, has concluded an agreement with VG WORT under which VG WORT annually transmits to the ALCS the money earned in German PLR by the works of ALCS members (apart from the 25 per cent which German law requires it to withhold for tax but which individual writers can recover by going through the prescribed formalities). This money the ALCS distributes to its members in the proportions designated by VG WORT in accordance with the spot-check conducted by VG WORT in German libraries (cf. 1.7). The payments made by VG WORT in 1980, 1981 and 1982 totalled £135,000. Thus British writer members of the ALCS were receiving annual PLR payments from Germany before any British PLR had been paid to anyone.

As a collecting society the ALCS is concerned to administer on behalf of its members literary rights of the kinds that can be effectively exercised only collectively (cf. 1.9). It is not a rival to the literary agents, whose concern is with rights that can be exercised on behalf of the individual. In Britain the ALCS took part in the negotiations, which by 1983 seemed on the verge of a satisfactory conclusion, to create an administrative apparatus for the collective exercise of the rights that exist under copyright for the control of reprography, including photocopying. It has concluded agreements with collecting societies overseas for the exercise of collective rights in various areas and is a member of the international federation of collecting societies, CISAC (Confédération Internationale des Sociétés d'Auteurs et Compositeurs).

A skeletal literary collecting society was established in Britain in 1973 on funds donated by some members of Writers Action Group (see further 6.3, 3). That company was later expanded, regularised and formalised, on money provided by a few WAG members, as the ALCS. The first chairman of the ALCS was Lord Willis (cf. 1.3), who in 1982 became its president. In 1980 the ALCS became secure under the joint protection of the Writers' Guild of Great Britain and the Society of Authors.

Membership of the ALCS is open to all writers. The Secretary-General is Mrs Elizabeth Thomas, whose acquaintance WAG made when she was 'special' (political) adviser to Michael Foot, MP, who, as deputy leader of the Labour Party, steered the PLR Act of 1979 past the filibuster and onto the statute book (cf. 1.3 and 6.3, 11).

The address of the ALCS is: 430 Edgware Road, London W2 1EH.

1.12 Reciprocity

The primary PLR legislation in Britain, the 1979 Act, lays down no conditions about the nationality and place of residence of the authors it entitles to be paid.

During the passage of the legislation through Parliament Lord Willis moved and carried in the House of Lords an amendment limiting payments of British PLR overseas to countries that operated a PLR system under which payments were made to British authors, but the government insisted that the amendment be reversed during the later parliamentary stages.

After the Act was passed, the government at first opined that the secondary legislation (the Scheme) would have no power to introduce a limitation. Eventually, however, it accepted the view of the writers' organisations, which was backed by Counsel's opinion, that to do so was within the powers given by the Act to the Scheme, and the 1982 Scheme introduced the nationality-plus-residence qualification. It did not, however, make the provision for reciprocal payments that the writers had sought.

By the time the 1982 Scheme was published, British members of the ALCS were already receiving PLR from West Germany (cf. 1.11), and it therefore became a matter of honour and urgency for the ALCS, the Writers' Guild and the Society of Authors to persuade the British government to amend the Scheme in a way that would immediately allow reciprocal payments from Britain to Germany, as well as making reciprocity possible with any other country that might in the future be prepared to operate it.

In 1982 the British government agreed to give sympathetic consideration to reciprocity, and intensive discussion began between the ALCS, VG WORT and the Registrar of PLR (Mr John Sumsion) towards devising a practical means of carrying it out.

The difficulties lay not only in the dozens of detailed discrepancies between the British PLR system and the system operated by VG WORT but in the radically different attitudes of the British and the German legislation to those details. The German legislation requires nothing of the recipient except that he should exercise his right through a recognised collecting society, which means in practice that he should empower VG WORT to administer his PLR. The form of that administration is left to the collecting society concerned. In Britain, on the other hand, the 1979 Act lays down that the right can be exercised only through registration by a Registrar appointed by the government, and the Scheme ordains in minute detail the rules of the system that the Registrar is obliged to administer.

It is probable that, under any reciprocal arrangement between Britain and VG WORT, British authors would be the net gainers.

German PLR is more generously funded than British, probably to a point that would offset the fact that VG WORT pays 55 per cent of the British author's PLR earnings into communal funds from which he cannot benefit (cf. 1.10 and 2.5).

VG WORT's payments are made to a wider spectrum of authors than British payments. Since the 1979 Act requires the author to apply for registration, the only authors who can be registered are those who apply during their lifetime. Posthumous PLR is paid in Britain to the heirs of authors who have been registered, but authors who die without being registered, including those who died before the PLR administration opened to receive applications for registration, can never be registered and their works can never earn British PLR. German PLR, by contrast, being conducted under copyright (creator's right) legislation, is paid on all works still in copyright. Moreover, copyright under German law lasts until 70 years after the author's death, whereas the posthumous duration of British PLR is, like the normal posthumous duration of British copyright, only 50 years. The payments of German PLR transmitted to ALCS members via VG WORT include payments to the estates of British authors who died before PLR was instituted in Germany.

Finally, the signs are that German library-users borrow more titles of British origin than British library-users borrow titles of German origin. So far as Britain is concerned, this generally agreed observation applies to borrowing habits from public libraries alone, and indeed only they are, under the 1979 Act, relevant to British PLR, whereas the spot-check conducted by VG WORT is drawn from libraries of all types (cf. 1.9). Were the British loans sample to be extended to include non-public libraries, the balance of borrowing between the two countries might shift slightly, but probably not substantially.

1.13 Who counts as an author (or a co-author)?

Any system that pays PLR on books has to decide how many people it is prepared to count as the authors of one title. It must also decide whose contribution is to count as authorship: the contribution only of an original writer or, where there is one, the contribution also of a translator or an illustrator?

On these, as on so many, questions the seven literary PLR systems in operation have made diverse decisions.

In some of the decisions, particularly on the second question, it is possible to trace two critical factors. How much influence could be exerted on the decision by a particular professional group, such as translators or illustrators? (That question is often tantamount to 'How far is the group organised?') And on whom did the influence have to be exerted?

In Sweden, for instance, although the sum paid per loan is determined by a vote in Parliament, the administration of PLR is governed by the board of the Swedish Authors' Fund (*Sveriges Författarfond*), on which representatives of authors' organisations outnumber persons appointed by the government by two to one. In Iceland PLR is administered by a committee of three, two of whom are nominated by the Icelandic authors' organisation.

Influencing bodies of this kind is clearly a different exercise from the influences that might be attempted in Britain, where PLR is administered by a Registrar appointed by the government but the Registrar has no power to make or change the rules, which are set out in extreme detail in the Scheme. Changes to the Scheme or the Act can be brought about only by parliamentary amendment. In effect, anyone wanting such an amendment to be made must convince the minister for the arts, and his civil servants, of its desirability. Even then, the amendment will be introduced only if the government allows the necessary parliamentary time.

The campaign that Writers Action Group began in 1972 with the double objective of securing PLR legislation and securing it in the form most useful to writers was addressed primarily to whichever government was in power, since only with government backing did any legislation stand a realistic chance of being passed, and secondarily to the general public and to librarians, whose opposition to PLR weighed heavily with the politicians and the civil servants. With the introduction of the first government PLR Bill in 1976, WAG directed much of its energy to winning support for the Bill among individual MPs. However, when the first attempt at government legislation failed towards the end of 1976 (cf. 1.3), there was no certainty that the government would try again. WAG therefore switched its persuasive efforts back to the government, and a PLR Bill was reintroduced largely thanks to the personal concern with PLR of the prime minister, James Callaghan, who received a group of WAG writers who asked to be allowed to plead with him, and of Michael Foot, who had long been a champion of PLR and was an early (1973) member of WAG.

The passage of the 1979 Act again re-directed the writers' efforts. The Labour government was replaced by a Conservative government, which was also committed to PLR and which had to set its civil servants the task of drafting the Scheme required by the Labour government's Act. The 1979 Act required that the Scheme should be prepared in consultation 'with representatives of authors and library authorities and of others who appear to be likely to be affected by it'. This gave the writers a say, though not a decisive say, in the Scheme, which was drafted by the Office of Arts and Libraries (OAL), the section of the Department of Education and Science presided over by the (junior) minister for the arts.

Although the OAL produced various outline suggestions on which it invited the writers to comment, the final drafting of the Scheme was a last-minute business during which the writers were under threat that, if they made major objections to the OAL's proposals, the timetable would slip yet further and it would not be possible to seek parliamentary approval of the Scheme within the lifetime of the current Parliament (or, the writers added, of many of the writers).

In requiring the Scheme to be drafted in consultation with 'authors', the 1979 Act did not say who was to be considered an author. It was, as a matter of fact, only during the drafting of the Scheme by the OAL that the OAL was persuaded by the organisations of illustrators that the Scheme should rule that illustrators as well as writers should count as authors.

The Danish PLR system pays only one author per title. No payment is made on titles of multiple authorship. As authors the Danish system recognises both original writers and (by a later addition to its rules) translators. Presumably there is no conflict between the recognition of translators and the restriction to one author per title since Danish PLR is paid only to Danes and it is improbable that a title would have both a Danish original writer and a Danish translator.

The Swedish system pays Swedish original writers, Swedish illustrators and (since 1961) Swedish translators. Translations, however, are registered only under the name of the original author. The sum a translation earns in PLR cannot, therefore, be paid to the translator but is paid into a solidarity fund. As in Iceland and Germany, Swedish PLR is associated with communal welfare and literary funds from which authors can benefit (a subject discussed further in 2.5). In Sweden and in Iceland, the proportion of the total PLR allocation that goes into the communal funds and the proportion that is paid out in PLR to individual authors are decided by Parliament, whereas in Germany the decision is made by the collecting society that administers PLR.

Since 1966 there has been in Sweden a fixed ratio between various payments. If x is the basic fee paid per loan of an original title, then the annual fee paid per title in reference stock is $4x$, since in Sweden it is reckoned that a lending volume is lent on average four times a year (cf. 1.8), the fee paid into the communal fund in respect of the loan of a translation is $x/3$ and the annual fee paid into the fund per translation in reference stock is $4x/3$. Although illustrators were eligible for PLR from the beginning, they were slow to exert their influence in the appropriate places and it was only in 1971 that they acquired a seat on the board that governs the fund and secured an increased share of the allocation.

Whereas the British system simply makes no payment on loans of titles that have more than the number of co-authors permitted by the rules, the sums of PLR that are earned in Sweden by titles that have more than three authors (the Swedish permitted number) apiece are paid into the communal fund.

Iceland, similarly, pays into the communal fund the sums earned by books with more than one author (the Icelandic permitted number) and books whose copyright-owner cannot, after three years, be traced. Payment to Icelandic translators is at half the rate paid to original authors per volume in the stock-census.

Under the system administered by VG WORT in Germany, 55 per cent of the total sum allocated to VG WORT for PLR is paid into communal social funds (cf. 1.10). The remainder is then divided according to the loans that show up in the spot-check (cf. 1.7). The publisher receives 30 per cent of the sum a title earns, the author 70 per cent. VG WORT makes no payment to illustrators, whose entitlement to PLR is administered by another collecting society, Bild-Kunst. VG WORT recognises only one original author per title but it pays a larger fee on a book with a translator than on one without. The extra, which is equivalent to 50 per cent of the author's fee, goes to the translator.

In New Zealand, where PLR is administered by the Department of Internal Affairs, no payment is made on a title that has more than two authors. Writers, visual artists and translators count as authors, and where a title has two authors within that sense of the word the payment earned by the title is divided equally between them. One of the two co-authors may claim his share of the payment even if the other is disqualified under the citizenship or residence requirement (cf. 1.10).

The administration of Australian PLR was at first (from

1974) conducted by the Department of the Prime Minister and Cabinet but was in 1976 transferred to the Australia Council. The system makes payment to Australian original writers, translators, editors and (provided they are entitled to royalties under the publishing contract) illustrators. It accepts up to three authors per title, provided they are named on the title-page or listed in the Australian National Bibliography. The payment earned by the title is divided in equal portions between its co-authors unless one of the claimants produces a publishing contract showing a different division of the royalties between them, in which case the PLR payment is divided in the same proportions as the royalties.

The rules laid down by the PLR Scheme of 1982 for the British PLR system recognise writers and illustrators, including, in most cases, photographers (see further 3.4), as authors, provided they are named on the title-page. Translators, editors and compilers are specifically excluded from counting as authors. The British system acknowledges up to three writers or illustrators as authors of one title and makes no payment on titles with more. The Scheme that received parliamentary approval in 1982 made an exception of encyclopaedias and dictionaries, which were not eligible for PLR if they had more than one author apiece. This discrimination provoked objections from the writers' organisations, and in March 1983 the minister for the arts placed before Parliament an amendment which came into force on 1 May 1983 and which, from a PLR point of view, permits encyclopaedias and dictionaries to have as many co-authors (namely three) as are permitted to other titles.

The rule that illustrators count as authors is so framed that it might suggest that a visual artist could claim PLR as the sole author of a book consisting wholly of pictures. Under the 1982 rules that is precluded by another provision, which requires that, to be eligible for PLR, a volume must contain at least 32 pages (or 24 of poetry or drama) and that, to count as a page towards the minimum number, a page must have at least half its area occupied by text, not illustration. Here too, however, the minister brought into force, in May 1983, an amendment to the Scheme under which all pages containing some printed matter, unless it is musical score, count towards the minimum number. Works made eligible by amendments approved in May 1983 would, if registered before 30 June 1983, stand to earn PLR during the first sampling period (see further 5.2).

1.14 The co-authorship rules in Britain

Unlike the other systems that are prepared to make payment to more than one person on a given title, the British PLR system does not name the proportions in which the sum earned by the title is to be divided. Instead, it requires that the co-authors, two or three as the case may be, should make a joint application for the registration of the joint title in which they state jointly what percentage of the PLR earned each co-author is to take. An application from one person for registration of a title is not accepted if the bibliographical records show that the title has in fact a co-author (writer or illustrator).

The co-authorship rules of the 1982 Scheme (which are discussed in greater detail in 3.5 and 3.7 – 3.10 and in 4.1) have several consequences detrimental to the writers and illustrators concerned. The ruling that an application for PLR must be made during the author's lifetime extends to the joint application required from co-authors, all of whom must be alive at the time of application. As a result, a writer who introduces and annotates a play by Shakespeare or an illustrator who illustrates one is for ever debarred from being paid PLR on his work, because his co-author, William Shakespeare, is dead. If a pair or a trio of living co-authors complete a work together but one of them dies between completion and registration, which cannot take place until the work has been published, then the survivors forfeit PLR for ever. Similarly, if co-authors, though alive, cannot get in touch with one another and therefore cannot make joint application, they all forfeit PLR.

The 1982 Scheme does, however, concede that, where a co-author is ineligible under the nationality-plus-residence qualification (cf. 1.10), the co-author who is (or the two co-authors who are) eligible may all the same receive PLR. Even in those circumstances, however, the application has to be a joint one by all the co-authors, including any who are ineligible, because only a joint application can, under the rules, specify the percentage of the earnings to be taken by a co-author who is eligible. Since, however, a co-author who is not eligible cannot earn any PLR himself, there is no financial incentive for him to take part in the joint application should he be lazy or uncharitable towards his colleagues.

The decision by the Office of Arts and Libraries (cf. 1.13) to require co-authors to state in a joint application what percentage of the PLR each was to take was prompted by the practical need to avoid occasions where the Registrar might have to adjudicate between co-authors squabbling over their shares.

However, the Registrar would have been protected just as effectively had the Scheme laid down the apportionment of the PLR between co-authors. A fixed division need not be so crude nor so cast-iron as to oblige co-authors to take equal shares in all cases, which, in a case where a co-author contributes only one page in a hundred would flout justice, and neither need the royalty split, which may well be influenced by considerations other than the importance of the contribution to the book, be the court of higher appeal (cf. 1.13). A fixed but flexible division of PLR between co-authors, proposed by the writers' unions, is recorded in 4.3.

In requiring the co-authors themselves to determine the share of each by agreement of all, the British government was acting on the principle of setting a thief to catch a thief: it decided to rely on the greed or self-interest of one co-author to counter the greed or self-interest of the other or others. This device does not work, however, when one co-author is ineligible for PLR, since he then has no financial interest in the division; and the fact that a dead co-author has no financial interest himself and cannot be a check on the self-interest of his colleagues has become the instrument of injustice to the survivors, since it simply abolishes their entitlement to PLR.

1.15 What counts as a book? Page requirements

The Scandinavian systems pay PLR without quibble on any literary work by an author of the required nationality that is (according to the method in use) lent from or stocked in the appropriate libraries.

By contrast, the New Zealand, Australian and British systems show symptoms of anxiety lest PLR should be paid on any work that is less than (to quote the British Office of Arts and Libraries) 'substantial'.

Accordingly, each of the three English-speaking systems operates a rule whereby no PLR payment is made on any work that does not contain a certain minimum number of pages. Each system stipulates its own minimum, which does not coincide with the minimum named by any of the others.

Whether a 'substantial' work is one that cost its author a substantial effort or one that provides a borrower with a substantial read has not been explained but is in any case irrelevant. The length of a work is not a measure of the work's substance in either of those senses. Moreover, the number of pages in the published format of a work is not a measure of its length.

For a writer it often, perhaps usually, takes more labour and thought to write succinctly than to write at length.

For the reader, whether the work provides him with a substantial read often depends on whether the writer has written succinctly or diffusely.

The authorised English translation of the *Manifesto of the Communist Party* runs to 48 pages. Even were the authors (Marx and Engels) still alive, the *Manifesto* would be ineligible for PLR under the minimum-page-number requirements of New Zealand, though not under those of Australia or Britain. Yet it would be impossible to maintain that it did not cost its authors a substantial amount of work and thought, that it does not provide a reader with a substantial amount of factual and analytical reading-matter or, indeed, that it has not had an extremely substantial effect on 20th-century ideas and history.

The poems by T. S. Eliot that were later gathered into one volume as *Four Quartets* were originally published as four separate works, in, respectively, 1940, 1941, 1941 and 1942, containing, respectively, ten, seven, nine and eight-and-a-third pages of verse. The poems have certainly made a substantial impact on the literature of the 20th century, but, were a living poet to publish them in the original format, the New Zealand, Australian and British PLR systems would unanimously rule that they could earn no PLR.

New Zealand and Australia operate the stock-census system, where an invariable shelf-fee is paid per volume stocked in the sample libraries. In these circumstances it can be argued that it would be unfair to a weighty volume were its presence in the libraries to earn it no more PLR than would be earned by a flimsy pamphlet. Even so, it is difficult to see why that argument should carry weight in a system where a volume with 25 borrowers a year earns no more PLR than a volume with no borrowers.

In any case, the method chosen to act on the argument is

incapable of doing what is expected of it.

A page can be of whatever size the publisher wants it to be. So can the typeface of the print that occupies it. A volume containing 22 large pages printed in small type, which would be ineligible for PLR under all three English-speaking systems, may contain ten times the quantity of words that is to be found in a volume of 50 small pages printed in a large typeface, which would be eligible to earn PLR under all three systems.

In making the possession of a certain number of pages a criterion of a work's eligibility to earn PLR, the three English-speaking systems have made eligibility depend not on the work's length, and still less on the intellectual content that the author put into it or a borrower can get out of it, but simply on the format in which the publisher has chosen to issue the author's work.

The idea of stipulating a minimum number of pages appears to have been imported from the Australasian systems into the British PLR Scheme of 1982 blindly – in, that is to say, disregard of the fact that the British PLR system, unlike the Australasian systems, is loans-based.

That fact itself equips the British system with another and much more reliable criterion of whether a work is 'substantial'. If a borrower chooses to take the work out of the library, his action declares that he considers that it will provide him (no matter what any other borrower or reader might think of it) with reading-matter substantial enough to justify him in borrowing it.

The borrower may be a slow reader, child or adult. He may have judged, before deciding to borrow the work, that it is one of those which, like the *Manifesto of the Communist Party*, is short in length but long in the digesting. His reasoning is inscrutable by the PLR system but his decision is recorded and should be, by the terms of a loans-based system, enough to score a PLR earning for the volume he picks.

In stock-census systems, to determine eligibility by a page count may be laudable in intention, in that it may be trying to compensate for other and grosser inequities in the system, but it cannot perform what is intended. In a loans-based system it merely substitutes an irrational and arbitrary criterion for the decision of the borrower.

A loans-based system, simply by being one, makes the borrower's decision the arbiter of what shall earn PLR and in what quantity. It is no more justified in over-ruling the borrower on the grounds that his choice has too few pages than it would be on the grounds, which also depend on a decision by the publisher, that it is not elegantly enough printed.

Under the rules of the New Zealand system, no payment is made on a volume unless it contains at least 50 pages of prose, 25 pages of verse or 100 pages of photographs or other pictures, though since 1975 the administrators of PLR have had a discretionary power to make certain payments on certain children's books that fail to meet the minimum-page requirement: if the title in question is a children's book that contains both text and illustrations, then, provided the volume contains at least 24 pages, 15 per cent of the PLR that the title earns may be paid to the writer and 15 per cent to the illustrator.

Australia applies the definitions of a book formulated by UNESCO. For a volume to earn PLR in Australia it must contain a minimum of 48 printed pages or 24 pages in the case of poetry, drama or children's books.

In Britain, the PLR Scheme of 1982 applies the UNESCO formulae but with modifications, thereby forfeiting the sole merit that could be claimed for them, namely that they are the formulations of an independent and international agency.

Under the 1982 rules, a volume cannot earn PLR in Britain unless it has a minimum of 32 pages or 24 pages in the case of poetry or drama.

Unlike Australia, Britain does not extend the lower minimum to children's books, because in drafting the Scheme (cf. 1.13) the Office of Arts and Libraries was afraid that to do so would leave the Registrar liable to embroilment in disputes about what was and what was not a children's book.

The details of the British page requirements are described in 3.15.

1.16 What counts as a book? Other criteria

Besides excluding volumes that do not contain the minimum number of pages stipulated in each case, the three English-speaking systems exclude from eligibility to earn PLR certain other categories of title or volume on grounds that are sometimes common to all three systems, sometimes common to two and sometimes unique.

These other exclusions are shown in Table 1.1. Some of the exclusions that are peculiar to New Zealand (for instance, 4,

15 and 17) show a pronounced tendency in the New Zealand PLR system to assimilate itself to copyright law.

Table 1.1 Exclusions (other than those on grounds of page numbers) from PLR under the rules of New Zealand (NZ), Australia (A) and Britain (GB).

Category Excluded	in		
1. unpublished titles	NZ		GB
2. volumes not printed and bound (but paperbacks count as bound); musical scores (since May 1983)			GB
3. titles that have not been offered for sale to the public (free handouts; titles before publication)			GB
4. titles in which copyright does not subsist	NZ		
5. serial publications (journals, magazines, &c.)	NZ	A	GB
6. titles not listed in the relevant National Bibliography	NZ	A	
7. encyclopaedias, dictionaries, &c. with more than one author (in relation to Britain see 1.13)		A	GB
8. titles whose author is a body corporate		A	GB
9. titles in Crown copyright	NZ	A	GB
10. titles without identifiable authorship		A	
11. titles first published more than 50 years before the PLR year in question, unless the author is still alive		A	
12. school text books	NZ		
13. compilations of sheet music, maps, tables, etc.	NZ		
14. local editions of works published overseas and not otherwise qualifying	NZ		
15. compilations where the copyright in the work as a whole subsists solely in 'the selection, arrangement, order or abridgement of the material constituting the work'	NZ		
16. volumes donated to libraries (cf. 1.6)	NZ		
17. works whose creation was commissioned and paid for 'in money or money's worth' and works that were created in the course of the author's employment 'under a contract of service or apprenticeship'	NZ		

This is particularly clear in the last-listed exclusion (17), which is modelled on the provision in the British copyright statute (and on similar provisions in other statutes that adopt the general concepts of British copyright) whereby the creator of the copyright work is not invariably the owner of the copyright in it (cf. 1.9).

Thus the British Copyright Act of 1956 (under subsections 2, 3 and 4 of section 4) provides that, unless there is an agreement to the contrary, (a) when a literary, dramatic or visually-artistic work is created in the course of the creator's employment by the proprietor of a newspaper or periodical 'under a contract of service or apprenticeship', then the copyright in respect of publication in a newspaper, periodical, etc. belongs to the proprietor of the newspaper etc. who employs the creator, (b) when a person commissions and pays for 'in money or money's worth' the creation of a photograph, a drawn or painted portrait or an engraving, then the copyright in the work belongs to the commissioner and (c) when, in any case not covered by the previous two provisions, the creator creates the work in the course of his employment 'under a contract of service or apprenticeship', then the copyright in the work belongs to the employer.

The New Zealand PLR system stops short of paying the PLR earned by the work to the person who commissioned the work or to the employer of the creator, but it deprives commissioned and employed authors of entitlement to PLR (which must discourage writers from accepting commissions from publishers for books) in much the same manner as British-type copyright law deprives some commissioned and employed creators of the copyright in their work.

A touch of the tendency of the New Zealand PLR system to mimic copyright is shown by the British PLR Act of 1979, which makes the posthumous duration of PLR identical with the normal posthumous duration of copyright under the 1956 Copyright Act (cf. 1.12).

All the same, PLR is not an aspect of copyright in either country or indeed in any country except West Germany, where the creator's right statute of 1965 safely puts the copyright in a work invariably, and indeed inalienably, in the possession of the work's creator (cf. 1.9).

The Australian PLR system and the British Scheme of 1982 originally shared (exclusion 7 in the table) a refusal to permit encyclopaedias and dictionaries to have, for PLR purposes, as many authors as other titles may have, though that rule was rescinded in 1983 so far as the British system was concerned (cf. 1.13). This eccentric rule has a curious appendix. Both the British and the Australian systems treat a title that is published in more than one volume as though it were so many separate titles, with the result that each volume of a work in several volumes can earn its own PLR, but Australia witholds this provision from encyclopaedias, which it treats as single titles, no matter how many volumes they run to.

1.17 Lower and upper limits

Systems (whether of PLR or anything else) that pay out large numbers of small sums are in danger of spending more on calculating and making the payment than the sum paid amounts to. Several PLR systems guard against that danger by limiting the smallness of the sums they are liable to pay out.

In New Zealand and Australia the limitation operates through the rule that no PLR is paid on a title unless the sample stock-census shows that there are probably at least 50 copies of the title in the libraries (cf. 1.6).

That method of limitation cannot be applied in a loans-based system, and in Sweden and Britain the lower limit is couched in terms of cash.

In Sweden the lower limit applies to the whole of an author's PLR earnings, that is, to the total earnings of all his titles if he has more than one, and no payment is made of any sum lower than SKr 150.

In Britain, the lower limit applies to the PLR earnings of a given edition of a given title, which means, in effect, to the earnings of one ISBN (cf. 1.4). If the earnings of one edition amount to less than the lower limit, the author receives no payment on that edition. In the Scheme of 1982 the lower limit is £5 per edition, but in 1983 the minister for the arts was contemplating seeking (in October 1983) to lower the threshold.

Iceland, although the system it operates is one based on a stock-census, also applies a bottom limit in terms of cash. A PLR earning of less than 300 kronur in a year is paid not to the individual author but into the communal fund.

Paradox enters PLR with the imposition of an upper limit – a limit, that is, on how large a sum can be paid out. Some form of limitation on PLR earnings is imposed by all loans-based systems. The paradox is that all loans-based systems go to some trouble and administrative expense, and some go to meticulous and expertly-devised lengths, to establish the precise sums earned in relation to borrowings; and then, having so carefully discovered the data, the loans-based systems set about systematically distorting the financial results that follow from them, at least in the upper reaches. It looks as though the legislators and administrators responsible for introducing loans-based PLR took the decision that the actions of the borrowers should be the determinant of how much PLR an author earned and then lost their nerve about the consequences.

No reason can be advanced in principle why an author who is massively popular with library-borrowers should not be paid the full amount of the PLR his popularity earns. In any state that does not place a rigid equivalent limit on the earnings, whether from private or public funds, of members of other professions, such as doctors, architects and managers of state-owned enterprises, the limitation on PLR earnings is bound to be read as a reflection of prejudice against the creators of books.

In practice, it can be argued that the money of which the upper limit deprives a popular author would probably, had it been paid him, have been taken away from him in income tax. That argument is not, however, applied to members of other professions, who are no less liable to income tax.

In Britain, where the PLR fund constitutes, after the deduction of expenses, a pool that is divided up between the authors in proportion to their loans (cf. 1.5), it can be further argued that a few popular authors would, if paid the full sums they earned, 'scoop the pool', with a consequent reduction in the rate paid per loan to everyone, with the result that the sums paid out to the less frequently borrowed authors would be reduced to insignificance. This argument is valid in practice, but only because the pool is inadequately funded in the first place.

The British is the only system that imposes its upper limit in the form of a crude ceiling. Under the PLR system of 1982, the largest sum that may be paid to any one author in any one year is £5,000.

The lower limit is applied per edition (per ISBN), but the Office of Arts and Libraries was dissuaded from applying the upper limit in the same way by the writers' organisations, who pointed out that to do so would enable prolific popular authors to 'scoop the pool' at the expense of less prolific authors both popular and unpopular.

As a result of the writers' argument, the upper limit in Britain operates per author. The earnings of each of an author's titles, including his percentage earnings on titles in co-authorship if he has any, his earnings under all his pseudonyms if he has any and the earnings of all works originally registered in his name even if he has now transferred ownership of the PLR in them to someone else (see further 2.6), are added together before the £5,000 ceiling is applied.

The sums that are chopped off the top of an author's PLR

earnings by the upper limit, together with the sums of less than £5 that are earned by editions but not paid because of the operation of the lower limit, are returned to the PLR pool.

Sweden, which does not fund PLR from a pool but names a sum to be paid per loan, operates a more refined limitation on PLR earnings. It takes the form of a tapered scale of rates of payment. This is applied to the total PLR earnings of each author. At the rates in force in 1974, the author was paid 10 öre for each loan in the first 100,000 loans he scored, 5 öre for each loan in his next 100,000 loans, 2 öre for each loan in his next 200,000 loans and 1 öre thereafter.

The method by which VG WORT calculates payments of German literary PLR combines a tapered scale with payment in bands.

Banded payment is in itself a device for saving accountancy and administration costs. If an enterprise is going to make three payments totalling £300, it is administratively cheaper to pay out three sums each of which consists of £100 than to pay out three sums of £101.09, £94.61 and £104.30. Payment in bands consists of bringing about the cheaper situation by artificial means.

Under the banded system operated by VG WORT, there are only nine distinct sums that can be paid, the lowest consisting of DM 84 and the highest of DM 8,400.

Each sum is then related to a span of numbers of loans that show up in the WORT spot-check of loans (cf. 1.7). The loans are counted per author, the loans of all an author's titles being added together to yield his total score in the spot-check. Any author whose total score is five loans or fewer is placed in the lowest band and is paid DM 84. Any author whose total of loans falls between six and ten is placed in the second band and earns the second sum, DM 168. The spot-check is too small to achieve enough accuracy for complaint to be made about the loss of accuracy occasioned by banding.

The payments, besides being banded, are weighted. That is to say, one band is weighted in relation to another. Instead of going up by even steps, the bands are biased in favour of the smaller numbers of loans. The higher the number of loans an author scores in the spot-check, the smaller the amount he is paid for each loan.

The top band contains in effect a ceiling, since the payment (DM 8,400) represents 501 or more loans in the spot-check, with the result that an author who scored 2,000 loans could not earn a larger sum than an author who scored 501.

The nine bands or categories operated by VG WORT are shown in Table 1.2.

Table 1.2

Band	Number of loans in spot-check	sum paid (DM)
I	5 or fewer	84
II	6 to 10	168
III	11 to 20	252
IV	21 to 30	336
V	31 to 50	504
VI	51 to 100	840
VII	101 to 250	1,680
VIII	251 to 500	4,200
IX	501 or more	8,400

2 Purposes and rationale

2.1 PLR: a fossil name

In Swedish the payment made to the author under the PLR system is called the *författarpenning:* literally, author's penny or author's coin. In German it is usually known as the *Bibliothekstantieme*, the library royalty.

A pedant might object to the application of the term 'royalty', which in a literary context normally connotes the author's percentage of the purchase-price of a volume, to something that is in fact a flat, if weighted, fee per borrowing (cf. 1.17). All the same, the German name does suggest a payment to an author and does connect it with libraries. Both the German and the Swedish names have the merit of giving anyone who hears them some notion of the type of transaction they mean. So have the Danish name, *Biblioteksafgift* (literally, library royalty) and the Icelandic name, *Höfundarettur* (literally, author's right).

The same cannot be claimed for the term 'Public Lending Right'. At best it is enigmatic. It loses nothing, except its unwieldiness, in being reduced to the inscrutable 'PLR'. To anyone who construes English in the normal way the name is likely to suggest that a right to lend is vested in the public, whereas in fact the right is vested in the author and consists of his right to payment when someone else lends his work to the public.

In Britain, a form of PLR was first suggested, under another name, in 1951. The suggestion, which is described further in 6.1, was made by my father, John Brophy, 1899–1965, a professional novelist, short-story writer, writer of non-fiction books and critic. My father persuaded the Society of Authors to take up the infant proposal and at some moment between 1951 and 1960 (when the name appeared in a book title) it was misnamed 'Public Lending Right'.

When Writers Action Group (WAG) was formed in 1972, many members sought a change in the name of what WAG was campaigning for. A postal ballot of the still small membership of WAG early in 1973 showed a strong majority in favour of renaming it 'Authors' Lending Right'. However, WAG was already in negotiation with a government and civil service in whose thoughts it was indelibly 'Public Lending Right', and

41

this was true not only of Britain but of governments and writers' organisations in New Zealand and Australia. By 1979 the thing itself had been administered or legislated into being in those three English-speaking countries, still under its misleading name.

The name is, as a matter of fact, a fossil. It dates from a period when British writers or lawyers contemplated (as, later, Australian writers briefly did) the introduction of PLR under copyright law, despite the disadvantages of that (cf. 1.9) to authors as such.

British copyright statutes, including that of 1956, which is still in force, proceed by naming the 'acts restricted by the copyright' in a work of a particular (literary, dramatic, musical or 'artistic') type. The actions that are 'restricted by the copyright' in a literary or dramatic work include reproducing the work in material form, publishing it, performing it in public and broadcasting it.

It is by this strangely oblique method that copyright legislation enables a copyright-owner to (sometimes) make money by means of his copyright. Since the actions named are 'restricted' (that is, forbidden in the absence of express permission), the owner of the copyright can raise money by charging someone a fee or a royalty in return for licensing him to do the otherwise forbidden action.

At some time during the 1950s it appeared that a simple method of instituting PLR would be by an amendment to the Copyright Act of 1956 that should add 'lending the work to the public' to the list of actions restricted by the copyright in a literary work.

It was this idea that shaped the name of Public Lending Right. The idea itself became extinct, but the fossilised name remained to mislead and sometimes mischievously mislead. The coinage intended to refer to 'lending to the public' by any type of library, but in the 1970s, when the PLR Bill was going through Parliament, its origin was so long forgotten that more than one politician mistakenly took the word 'public' in 'Public Lending Right' to mean that PLR was by definition confined to public libraries (cf. 1.9).

The idea of PLR-through-copyright became extinct because it was ill adapted to its environment, namely the climate of British (or, in the Australian case, British-type) copyright law. As a method of making just payment to authors (and thereby helping to keep a living literature alive and to continue the supply of contemporary reading-matter to borrowers from libraries), it was wobbly in its aim, since the copyright-owner who would have been the beneficiary is not necessarily identical with the author.

In addition to the instances (which are listed in 1.16) where it does not make the creator the owner of the copyright in his work in the first place, British copyright law, unlike French and German, allows the creator, if he does own the copyright, to assign it totally to someone else. The extreme poverty of large numbers of British writers makes them vulnerable to pressure to do so. A freelance writer who has just supported himself for a year while he writes a book is usually in urgent need of some cash return on his investment to enable him to stay alive to write another. If a publisher offers to publish the book but only on condition that the author assign the copyright to the publisher, the author may be too poor to refuse, since to seek another publisher might cost him months without income from the work he has done and failure to find another publisher would mean that he would never see any return on it.

To some authors of titles lent from libraries in Britain, therefore, PLR-through-copyright would have brought no payment. To the copyright-owners (a mixture, in unknown proportions, of authors, heirs and assigns, publishers and employers), it would have given no administrative apparatus for gathering the necessary data from the libraries and perhaps no statutory authority to do so. Unless a government had stepped in (as government sources do in Germany, where PLR depends on copyright) with an allocation of public funds, the copyright-owners would have had to seek their payment from the libraries themselves, who would probably have thereupon reduced their purchases of books.

In Britain, an unsuccessful attempt to introduce PLR by amendment of the 1956 Copyright Act was made, in a private Member's Bill, as late as 1974. It was, however, anachronistic. The defects of copyright as a vehicle for PLR were already clear and the notion of PLR-through-copyright had been abandoned by the active section of the PLR campaign, leaving nothing but a misnomer behind it.

Bizarrely, the Act of 1979, which creates PLR as an independent right for authors, with no connexion with copyright, creates it under a name that makes sense only in the context of copyright.

2.2 Legislation or administrative arrangement?

The Danish copyright statute expressly says that it places no restriction on PLR, but PLR operates in Denmark under the legislative authority not of copyright but of the libraries statute of 1975. In Sweden the rates of PLR depend on Parliament, but the administration is conducted by the Swedish Authors' Fund (*Sveriges Författarfond*), on whose governing body representatives of authors outnumber those of government. PLR in Iceland was inaugurated under Law no. 22 of 1963 on public libraries and is continued under Law no. 50 of 1976, also on public libraries. These Laws specify, in terms of a percentage of their spending on libraries, the amounts to be contributed to the PLR fund by central and local governments, and place the administration of the fund in the control of a committee on which nominees of the authors' organisation predominate. German PLR rests on the authority of the creator's right (*Urheberrecht*) statute, which, however, requires PLR to be exercised through a collecting society. In Britain PLR was newly and expressly created as a right for authors by the 1979 Act and is administered by an apparatus which, though not an arm of the civil service, is a creation of government.

In New Zealand and Australia, however, PLR was instituted not by legislation but by the decision of a particular government or even, as in the case of Mr Gough Whitlam in Australia, of a particular prime minister. In New Zealand PLR is administered by the Department of Internal Affairs, in Australia by the Australia Council; the Act of 1975 which established the Council was amended in 1976 to include PLR among the Council's functions. PLR-by-'administrative-arrangement' has evident dangers, since it would be easier to rescind a government decision than to go through the long process of repealing a statute, but the administrative arrangements so far made have been upheld by successor governments.

Whether PLR requires legislation and, if so, of what kind is dictated by local circumstance. The telling factors include the attitude to PLR of the librarians and also the degree of co-operation that the system intends to ask of them.

In 1969, when the Swedish authors were campaigning for an increase in their rates of PLR payment, one of the causes of their success was that they had the support of the librarians for their legendary 'library action'.

That action, which took place on 23 April 1969, became, in the following decade, an inspiration to Writers Action Group in Britain – whose campaign for the institution of PLR could not, however, make use of the Swedish authors' device, because the libraries in Britain operate different regulations from the Swedish. A book ticket for a public library in Britain is usually local to the district where the ticket-holder lives, works or is being educated (see further 2.3), and it normally permits him to borrow no more than six volumes at a time. A Swedish ticket entitles the holder to borrow an unlimited number of volumes from any public library in Sweden. Swedish authors were therefore able to make their protest by, on the appointed day, virtually emptying the main libraries in the main cities of Swedish books (the only ones to which Swedish PLR is relevant), an action that broke no law and that had, in many cases, the help of the librarians.

By contrast, the Library Association in Britain was, to an extent unmatched in any country that has PLR, vehemently and officially opposed to the introduction of PLR. There were, however, several librarians who as individuals gave their support to PLR and to Writers Action Group.

In effect, the Library Association compelled the British government to introduce legislation giving the Registrar of PLR power to require the local library authorities to provide him with the data needed for the operation of PLR. Evidently the Library Association judged it preferable that public libraries be compelled by statute to take part in the loans sample than that the Library Association should reach an agreement with the government.

While the campaign for PLR in Britain was still inchoate and the government had not yet committed itself to legislation in any form, the librarians had two legitimate sources of worry: how much extra work (and of what type and how paid for) would be required of the people who worked in libraries; and would the money to pay PLR come from a source that could lessen the libraries' own funds, thereby impairing the public-library service and reducing the power, and ultimately the manpower, of the library profession?

Writers Action Group was formed in 1972 with a policy of loans-sampling (which would impinge on only a small percentage of libraries) by automated means (that would not be onerous to librarians or library assistants) and a programme

45

that stipulated that PLR should be paid from central government funds and should therefore not touch the libraries' book funds, which would have been as much against the writers' as the librarians' interest.

In January 1974 the Library Association told Maureen Duffy and me, the organisers of Writers Action Group, that it intended to diminish and eventually to cease its opposition to PLR. The prediction did not come true, and the Library Association maintained its hostility to PLR even after the introduction of legislation incorporating the main items of WAG policy.

The two most widely-based and accurate loans samples, those taken in Britain and in Sweden, depend on the provision of extensive data by the libraries (cf. 1.7), and that in turn must depend either on a statutory obligation to provide them or on the good will of librarians or on both. Similarly, the most comprehensive stock-censuses are those taken in Denmark and in Iceland (cf. 1.6), where PLR is administered under the same statute as the libraries.

On the other hand, in New Zealand and Australia, where PLR rests on ministerial rather than statutory authority, the stock-census is a matter of comparatively infrequent stock-sampling. In Germany, the spot-check data that are the basis for the distribution of PLR by VG WORT are not provided by libraries but are obtained by VG WORT itself. It is possible that the PLR legislation in the creator's right statute does not give the collecting societies sufficient authority to require the libraries to provide data or it may be that there is no pressure from the authors whose PLR is administered (cf. 1.7) for the collection of more than the scantiest of samples.

The surprise often expressed in Germany that Britain chose to introduce PLR by a method other than copyright legislation rests perhaps on ignorance, perhaps on incredulity, of the fact that under British copyright law the copyright-owners are not in all cases identical with the authors and their heirs. Neither was there, in the early 1980s, much prospect of copyright reform. The Whitford Committee, which reviewed British copyright law in 1977, did not recommend anything to make creators less vulnerable to dispossession of the copyrights they do possess and neither did it recommend any substantial change in the instances (cf. 1.16) where the Copyright Act of 1956 does not make the creator the owner of the copyright in the first place. A 'consultative document' issued in 1981 by the

Department of Trade as a follow-up to Whitford included a suggestion that would, if acted on, increase the number of creators who never own the copyright in their creations, since it proposed that the copyright in a commissioned work should always vest in the commissioner. Since most professional writers accept commissions from publishers in return for a fraction of the advance, in order to finance the writing of the book, that suggestion would divest a high proportion, perhaps the majority, of professional writers of the copyright in their books and, had PLR been introduced under copyright, of their PLR as well.

Despite the disadvantages to authors in countries, of which there are several, whose copyright law separates the author from the copyright-owner, there is some propagandist pressure in Europe, and particularly in the EEC, for future PLR systems to be introduced under, and even for existing ones to be switched to, copyright law. In theory that would make it easier to create an international network of PLR systems paying one another's authors reciprocally, though it would not remove the difficulties in practice caused by the discrepancies between existing systems. The same consideration makes governments shy away from PLR-through-copyright, which would necessarily be international, especially governments whose libraries make heavy use of foreign works, whether in translation or in an overseas version of the native language, because such governments are bound to suspect that in an international PLR network they would be net losers (cf. 1.12).

Even in countries whose copyright consists impeccably of creator's right, copyright is not necessarily the perfectly fitting slot for PLR that its propagandists suggest. It may leave open the practical question of an administrative apparatus, which may have to be established by other means under separate legislation, as it is in Germany, where the collecting societies provide the apparatus, and it raises a doubt whether copyright legislation, which is notoriously difficult to enforce, can confer the authority necessary to requiring the libraries to provide exhaustive data.

Even doctrinally, PLR does not fit into a copyright framework unless it is treated as an exception to the general copyright concept of the 'exhaustion of rights', according to which, when a copyright-owner has taken money for the disposal of the copyright work, as the author has by the sale of a volume to a library, he possesses no further rights in it. To this concept PLR has to form an exception along with *droit de suite*, the right of the creator of a work of visual art (or of a literary or musical manuscript) to a share in the proceeds of any re-sale (after the creator's first sale to the first owner) of the work or manuscript. *Droit de suite* operates in France and Belgium and is recognised in principle in Germany, Italy and Scandinavia. It is allowed for by, but is not obligatory under, the Berne Copyright Convention.

Thus there are advantages both practical and theoretical in simply treating the 20th-century growth of library lending in industrial societies as an historical phenomenon whose consequences affect authors of books and in taking legislative measures designed to meet the particular problem rather than seeking a solution that will fit into an existing corpus of theory and practice.

2.3 The crisis for authors

Although suggestions for PLR are said to have been put forward in Germany during the 19th century and were certainly discussed by the Swedish Authors' Association in 1933, the problem that authors seek to solve by PLR seems to have become acute after the war of 1939–45.

Commercial lending libraries came into existence during the 18th century. Books were then comparatively more costly than they became in the 20th, and the libraries were a direct response to the desire of the upper and middle class to read more of them than they could afford to buy. Commercial libraries paid their way and hoped to make a profit for their proprietors by charging borrowers a subscription.

Jane Austen was solicited to subscribe to a library of this kind in 1798. 'As an inducement to subscribe', she reported to her sister, 'Mrs. Martin tells us that her Collection is not to consist only of Novels, but of every kind of Literature, etc. etc. – She might have spared this pretension to *our* family, who are great Novel-readers and not ashamed of being so; – but it was necessary I suppose to the self-consequence of half her Subscribers.'

In Britain the commercial libraries developed into such large Victorian institutions as Mudie's and, later, such huge high-street chains as the Boots and W.H. Smith's libraries. Neither in Britain nor elsewhere was the commercial development inhibited by the institution of 'free' (to the borrower) libraries, because the two types of library addressed themselves to different publics. The 'free' libraries in Britain (cf. 1.9) were designed for the working class and, during the 19th century, concentrated on instructional or at least 'improving' reading-matter. The commercial libraries addressed the middle class from whom subscriptions could be collected and for whom they provided not only fiction but entertainment, camouflaged though the latter might be in deference to the 'self-consequence' of the subscribers or, presently, to the censorious observance of the Victorian decencies.

In Britain it was certainly the war of 1939–45 that wrought the triumph of the public over the commercial libraries. Thitherto the middle class had eschewed the 'free' libraries, whether in disdain of 'charity' or in the belief that pages turned by proletarian fingers were liable to transmit disease. Wartime Britain, however, was an egalitarian society (one person, one ration book). Remembered in the 1980s it could present an ideal ('The best example that I've seen of Democratic Socialism operating in this country was during the Second World War' – Michael Foot, 1982, quoted in the *Guardian*, 6 December); and at the time it laid down plans for the future creation of the welfare state, with the publication, in December 1942, of the Beveridge Report, in which the committee chaired by Sir William (later Lord) Beveridge recommended welfare benefits financed by social insurance. Experience of wartime Britain broke down both the pride and the superstitions that had kept the middle class out of the public libraries, and at the same time it put into middle-class heads the notion that it was silly to pay for something that the state provided free or, rather, that the taxpayer had to pay for in any case.

Once the war was over, the public-library network set out on what proved a huge and rapid programme of expansion. At the same time it abandoned whatever shreds remained of its policy of providing mainly instructive material, a change of heart that must have made it more attractive to its old working-class as well as its new middle-class clientele and that was essential if book-borrowing was not to be overtaken by the mass entertainments of radio and television. A few public librarians remained as philistine and puritanical as the Mrs Martin who solicited Jane Austen, but by 1974–5 virtually 71 per cent of all loans of books for adults from the public-library network as a whole were loans of fiction.

By then commercial libraries were virtually extinct. Mudie's closed after its stock was destroyed by bombing during the war. The Smith's and Boots chains held out until the 1960s, but falteringly.

In this history I think it is possible to discern one of the points where the crisis began to tighten on authors, whose earnings depend, in the absence of PLR, on the number of copies sold of their work. The commercial libraries were in competition with one another. J. A. Sutherland speaks of 'years of internal competition, especially in London, between Smith's, the Times Library, Harrods, Mudies and Boots'. This, he correctly says, weakened the commercial libraries' power to resist the advance of the public libraries. However, it must have done so by maximising the number of copies that the commercial libraries bought, since each library must have hoped to be able to offer its customers swifter and more up-to-date access than its rivals could to recent titles, of which the commercial libraries often bought multiple copies.

The public libraries, by contrast, were not and are not in competition with one another. Indeed, so far as borrowers are concerned, each district constitutes a local monopoly (cf. 2.2). The Public Libraries and Museums Act requires (under section 7) the local library authorities to provide a library service for all persons desiring to use it, but, although the Act permits an authority to provide a service literally 'for all persons', it specifically does not place the authority 'under a duty' to provide a service for anyone except those persons living, working or being educated 'within the library area of the authority'.

The relation of one public library to another is, accordingly, not competitive but co-operative. A public library may buy more than one copy of a popular title, but there is no financial or competitive pressure on it not to keep borrowers waiting for the title they want. In practice, reservations create a waiting list. A request for an esoteric title is likely to prompt a public library not to buy a copy but to borrow one from another public library.

At a guess, lending libraries became an acute threat to authors' incomes when the competitive commercial libraries, whose competitiveness maximised their purchases even to the ruin of their own economies as profit-seeking concerns, were replaced by the public libraries, whose organisation and ethos

50

were directed to saving the ratepayers' money.

2.4 Rationale: compensation or payment for service?

By the 1960s the public libraries in Britain had completed their victory over the commercial libraries and were accepted by all classes of the citizens as an aspect of the welfare state. It was widely assumed that the state had the duty of educating the infant and teaching him to read. It was almost universally assumed that to the state fell the duty of keeping him supplied with reading-matter for ever after. Indeed, it was with precisely that implication that the Public Libraries and Museums Act of 1964 placed on the local authorities the duty of providing a library service for all persons in their area 'desiring to make use thereof'.

By 1974 the public-library network consisted of 6,500 (or 12,500 if those in hospitals, etc. were included) 'service points', a term covering every source from which books are issued, from major library to mobile van.

In the year 1969–70, the public libraries in Britain made a total of 656 million book loans, a stupendous total compared with the figures for any other western country, especially given that public libraries are by no means the only libraries making loans. In 1972–3 the annual total began to fall, but by the year 1979–80 it was again in excess of 650 million, and in the year 1981–2 it was over 661 million.

These totals are reached by adding together the totals which the Municipal Year Book elicits by questionnaire from the 165 library authorities and boards. The figures are seldom complete. Those for 1981–2 contain no returns for book issues from four of the 165 authorities. Most of the returns clearly purport to be exact counts (e.g. 2,812,998) but a few look like round approximations (e.g. 2,000,000).

A volume on the open lending shelves of a public library in Britain, it was reckoned in 1974, was on average borrowed seven times a year (in comparison with the Swedish average of four times a year and a West German estimate of four-and-a-half) and had a library life of, on average, 5.6 years. In other words, the average public-library volume in Britain served between 39 and 40 borrowers.

To many authors it seemed and seems that the high frequency of borrowing by the public must diminish the sales of

51

volumes to individual members of the public. The crisis that began to tighten on authors' incomes when the commercial libraries were ousted by local-monopoly public libraries seemed to be given several further twists when the public libraries expanded into a huge lending industry that penetrated every cranny of the country both geographically and socially.

Throughout the 1960s and 1970s, authors in Britain were aware that fewer and fewer of them were able to make a living from writing books, an impression confirmed by those who belonged to, and answered a questionnaire from, the Society of Authors in 1965.

The number of copies a title must expect to sell in paperback before a mass-market paperback publisher would take it on for paperback publication rose; but the number of copies sold that was sufficient to rank a hardback as a bestseller dropped (from, according to a British publisher quoted by Per Gedin, 35,000 in 1958 to 15,000 in 1973).

By the end of the 1970s, many hardback titles, notably hardback fiction not of bestseller status, achieved no sales through bookshops at all, the entire sale, usually of between 1,000 and 2,000 copies, being to public libraries. In those circumstances many writers were bound to believe that, had the public libraries not existed, at least five per cent of the borrowers of the average library volume would have bought a copy instead of borrowing one; and if only two out of the average 40 borrowers had done so, the author's earnings would have doubled.

Books are the only commodity that can be borrowed free by any member of the public. There is therefore no instant comparison to hand by which to judge what effect the easy availability of a free loan makes on the appetite to buy and possess.

That it at least may diminish that appetite is, however, accepted in many countries. In Australia it constitutes the official rationale of PLR. According to the Australia Council's booklet on PLR, authors and publishers are 'recompensed' by PLR in 'recognition of the fact that authors and publishers may lose income when readers do not have to buy books they want to read because those books can be borrowed freely from a library'.

Some of the advocates of PLR in Britain put forward the same rationale, and enemies of PLR often assume it to be one of the centres of the claim. 'At the centre of this argument', says an anti-PLR document issued by the Library Association in 1974, 'lies the opinion that the availability of books in libraries adversely affects the sale of these books, as a consequence of which the author's potential income is seriously reduced'.

Writers Action Group, formed in 1972, was careful to advance a claim only for payment for service. It was that claim that was pressed by the government in its explanations of the need for the 1979 Act. Officially, therefore, the rationale of PLR in Britain is that PLR is paid to originators of books in recognition of the fact that loans from public libraries serve between 550 and 650 million borrowers a year (and very often the borrower's family and immediate friends as well).

As a matter of fact, the service performed is not only to borrowers. By providing its raw material of books, authors keep in being a lending industry, dispersed throughout the country, that gives employment to some 24,000 people. This last figure does not include the employees of non-public libraries or manual employees of public libraries. During the year 1981–2, the public libraries in the United Kingdom employed a total of 8,182 qualified librarians and 16,606 assistants.

It is, of course, impossible to establish conclusively what people would have done had circumstances been different. It might be that, if no public libraries existed to provide them with reading-matter free and easily, the inhabitants of the British Isles would give up reading books and would instead spend all their spare time watching television or drinking, neither of which entertainments is, however, provided without charge to the consumer. Yet it is possible to make comparisons between Britain and other industrialised countries in Europe where there is an equal number of alternative pastimes available to the inhabitants but where the book-lending industry has not reached the colossal size it has in Britain. Such comparisons often suggest that the size and, perhaps more critically, the universal availability of the public libraries in Britain have triumphed not only over the commercial libraries but over the bookshops, with a consequent depressive effect on authors' incomes and the book trade. Books are the only commodity that retailers try to sell in competition with the free lending of the same commodity by the state.

A comparison between Britain and Germany does not show what must happen if, in two otherwise similar countries, there is a great discrepancy in the sizes of their library networks. It does, however, show what can happen; and that in itself is enough to refute some of the extravagant counter-claims put forward in Britain to the effect that the existence of the public libraries on so large a scale, far from damaging authors, benefits them.

The Federal Republic of Germany, with a population slightly larger than Britain's (62 million compared to 56 million), makes less than a third of the number of library loans. The number of loans made annually in Germany, from libraries of all types taken together, climbed during the 1960s and 1970s from 80 million to an estimated 210 million in 1982, which contrasts with the more than 650 million loans in the year 1979–80 from public libraries in Britain, plus an unknown but substantial number from non-public libraries.

These contrasting sizes of library industry apparently make contrasting effects on bookshops, though 'bookshop' is a term with various meanings. Britain was estimated in 1978 to have 30,000 outlets for the sale of paperbacks, but these, which include newsagents, confectioners, supermarkets, etc., carried only a section of the range of paperback titles in print, a range that itself constantly narrowed, during the 1970s, in the type of title that was accorded mass-market circulation.

Of shops that carry a representative range of hardback titles and are willing to order a title they do not carry for a customer willing to buy it sight unseen, Britain did not, between 1974 and 1983, possess more than 3,000 and probably possessed considerably fewer. In contrast, West Germany (according to the *Bookseller* of 30 October 1976) possessed in 1976 about 6,000 bookshops selling books and magazines exclusively – almost as many bookshops, that is, as Britain possessed public-library 'service points'.

Peter Mann's study, of 1975, of Yorkshire bookshops showed large areas, including industrial areas of high population, without ready access to a bookshop. A discussion paper on literature prepared for the Greater London Arts Association in February 1978 included a plan of London (Camden to Lewisham, Hammersmith to Greenwich) on which it marked 41 'general stockholding' bookshops; in contrast it cited Munich and West Berlin, neither of which has a population as large as London's, as possessing, respectively, 244 and 263 bookshops.

As a result of the contrast in numbers of bookshops, the turnover in 1974 of West German publishers, on books and specialist (but not general) magazines, was three to four times higher than the turnover of British publishers on books – and that despite the absence of a German-language export market to match the valuable English-language export market, which in 1974 accounted for 36.7 per cent of British publishers' sales of books.

What is true of turnover is true also of the number of titles produced. In 1971, when the West German library service was still very small, making about 80 million loans a year from libraries of all kinds taken together, whereas Britain was at that date making 628 million loans a year from public libraries alone, West German publishers produced 42,957 titles, British publishers 32,538.

This suggests that the claim (advanced by the Library Association in Britain in 1974) that 'benefits. . . accrue to publishing and writing through the existence of the library market, which makes possible the publication of most of the books which reach print' resembles a claim that your artificial leg is of great benefit to you advanced by the person who cut off your natural one. It is true that the libraries make it possible to publish books, but only in the sense that the libraries have largely replaced the bookshops. In Germany, where a comparatively small library service has left the bookshops intact, the bookshops are capable of producing greater 'benefits' and of making possible the publication of a larger number of titles than the libraries do in Britain.

If the claim were true that the libraries in Britain 'underwrite' the publisher's risk and thus make possible the publication of titles not expected to be bestsellers, it would be vindicated in the number of fiction titles published, since the public libraries are the largest section of the lending industry and fiction-lending is the largest section of their activities. In 1974–5 fiction accounted for 70.9 per cent, in 1980–1 for 73.7 per cent of public-library loans of adult books. (Where loans of children's books are concerned, the figures issued by the Chartered Institute of Public Finance and Accountancy, from which these percentages are calculated, do not distinguish between fiction and non-fiction, but the predominance of fiction is unlikely to be smaller there.) The claim seems, however, to be contradicted by the history of fiction-publishing in Britain when that is compared with the history of the expansion of the public libraries.

The number of titles of all kinds published annually in

Britain has, with minor dips between one year and the next, been rising since 1900. A table published in the *Bookseller* of 1 and 8 January 1983 for the postwar years shows a more or less steady increase. In 1947 the total number of titles of all kinds produced in Britain was 13,046; in 1957, 20,719; in 1967, 29,619; in 1977, 36,322.

The number of fiction titles, however, was higher in 1937 (5,097) than in 1960 (4,209). By 1975, it had dropped to 4,198.

The 1960s and 1970s, when the annual number of fiction titles published was shrinking, coincided with the maximum number of loans made from public libraries, the major part of them loans of fiction.

Those years coincided also with large increases in the annual numbers of titles of all kinds, with the result that fiction's share of the total number of titles dropped: from about 22 per cent in 1937 to about 11 per cent in 1977. As between 1981 and 1982, there was a small increase (from 4,747 to 4,879) in the number of fiction titles published, but since there was a large increase in the number of titles of all kinds (from 43,083 in 1981 to 48,307 in 1982) fiction's proportion of the total of titles actually dropped from 11.01 per cent in 1981 to 10.09 per cent in 1982.

The claim that in Britain many books 'are produced primarily for the library market' may well be true, the libraries having left little other market, but the claim that such books are 'highly priced accordingly' is refuted by the case of fiction, the chief public-library commodity. On average, during the first six months of 1977, the price of a new hardback title (fiction and non-fiction averaged together) was £6.71, but the price of a new hardback fiction title was on average £3.49. In 1982 Michael Legat reported that there was still 'a convention within the trade and among the public that fiction should cost less than a non-fiction book of similar length and size. The novel that is currently priced at £6.95 would probably cost £8.95 or more if it were, say, a biography, even without illustrations.'

The claim that 'library services provide the best and cheapest shop-window available to the book trade' prompts authors to reply that a shop-window is no help to their incomes if there is no shop behind it. Since 1973, authors (including, notably, Maureen Duffy and Michael Holroyd) have taken the Library Association at its word and campaigned for the installation of actual bookshops on public-library premises, a campaign that has met some legal uncertainties as well as much inertia. By 1982, at least two such bookshops existed, at Shoreditch and Stamford Hill public libraries in London (letter in the *Bookseller* of 13 November 1982), and the Arts Council had funded a pilot scheme in Suffolk whereby Suffolk public libraries accepted and passed on to local booksellers orders for books. The funding was, however, adequate only to sounding out whether such a service was felt to be needed, not to advertising or promoting the service. A report of a one-day conference on the subject of bookshops and ordering services in public libraries was published in the *Bookseller* of 20 November 1982.

2.5 Social purposes

If part of the crisis for authors was caused by the decision of postwar industrialised societies to treat the publicly funded lending of books as an aspect of the welfare state, then there is a touch of poetic justice in the fact that three countries, Sweden, Iceland and West Germany, have combined the funding of PLR with the funding of repair work to gaps in the welfare fabric where it touches authors.

Professional, full-time writers count, in terms of welfare provision, as 'self-employed'. This means that, wherever a health-insurance or a pension contribution is normally paid jointly by employee and employer, writers, though their incomes are as a rule lower than those of other 'self-employed' people, have to pay both portions themselves and do not in all cases stand to claim all the benefits.

In Britain, however, the Writers' Guild has uniquely negotiated with the television companies a scheme, founded in 1975, whereby, when a Guild member is paid for a television script, four per cent of his fee is put into a pension fund in his name and a contribution of six per cent (additional to the fee itself) is added by the television company.

Because he is not technically an 'employee', a freelance writer is not eligible for unemployment benefit even when his services are not wanted by a publisher; he is not entitled to sickness benefit when he is ill and cannot pursue his work; and if a publisher, after publishing a book a year by him for 40 years, suddenly drops him, he is not protected by any of the general legislation governing unfair dismissal and redundancy payments that in developed postwar societies protects employees.

From the time (1954) that the Swedish Parliament first voted a PLR allocation, it required the money to be divided between payments to individual authors in proportion to their numbers of library loans and payments into a solidarity fund for authors. By the mid-1970s, PLR payments accounted for about a quarter of the total sum, payments into the solidarity fund for about three-quarters.

The Swedish solidarity fund provides supplementary payments to established freelance ('self-employed') authors whose PLR earnings do not, to the committee's mind, equal their literary importance; pensions; five-year (prolongable) grants to young authors; working and travel scholarships; awards; assistance to authors in need; and collective trade union dues.

By the Law of 1963 under which Icelandic PLR began, 60 per cent of the sum allocated was distributed to Icelandic authors in PLR payments and 40 per cent paid into funds for communal purposes. Under the revised Law of 1976, those proportions shifted to 50 per cent and 50 per cent. The content of the fund is spent on awards 'to individual authors as a recognition of their work' (to quote the Law of 1976), and translators are eligible for awards as well as original writers.

The payment of part of the PLR allocation in West Germany into social funds is not required by the PLR Article of the creator's right statute. It is permitted, though again not required, by the legislation on collecting societies.

VG WORT, the literary collecting society which receives 91.2 per cent of the sum allocated to PLR by the Federal and regional governments, is controlled by its members, who number only about 350 although VG WORT handles PLR and other rights for some 25,000 writers. Membership is confined to writers whose earnings through VG WORT are exceptionally high and who are prepared to enter a long-term agreement with VG WORT. It is the controlling membership of VG WORT who took the decision that, of the total sum allocated to PLR on general books, 45 per cent should be distributed to the writers whose PLR is administered and 55 per cent go into funds. Ten per cent is paid into a social fund, from which payments are made *ex gratia* to ill or elderly authors in need, and 45 per cent into a social security fund, from which professional writers (those who derive more than 50 per cent of their income from writing) can receive half their monthly pension or insurance contributions up to a maximum of DM 350. Non-German authors cannot benefit from either fund.

The Swedish and the Icelandic are the only national PLR systems, and the German collecting societies the only independent agencies, that divert part of the public money provided for PLR into collective funds designed to provide welfare benefits for 'self-employed' authors, sometimes subject to need or literary merit. Perhaps it is only in those countries that PLR is largely enough funded to perform two tasks, and that in turn no doubt reflects the value that the legislators set on the continuation of a native literature.

That is not to say, however, that the pure PLR systems, and in particular the British loans-based system, are without social purpose in relation to authors. True, the British PLR system can do nothing for writers whose work the public does not borrow from libraries. Stock-census systems pay PLR even if the public does not borrow, but not if the librarians do not buy. The Swedish solidarity fund augments the earnings of writers with few borrowers but, in the committee's view, much merit – a task that in Britain falls to, though it is not always discharged by, the Arts Council.

Whereas employment (or even unemployment) brings in a regular income (or at least a regular pittance), the sharpest cause of anxiety for the 'self-employed' writer, especially if he has a family to support, is that his bills arrive regularly but his income doesn't, even when he works regularly (and long, as he is likely to do, since social legislation that limits working hours has no application to him and weekends and public holidays no significance). Because he always has bills to catch up with, the pressure on the 'self-employed' writer is always towards the production of new work. It is this pressure that a PLR system can – or could, were it adequately funded – relieve, because it pays, only a year in arrears, for current use of past work. In the 1970s most titles published in Britain earned the major, perhaps the only, part of their income from royalties on sales within six or even three months of publication. In the libraries, however, a title may continue to be read fairly intensively for years, and a PLR system that reflects that fact in terms of adequate payments that continue so long as the title continues to be read can buy the writer time to rest or to be ill, thus giving him social benefits that are taken for granted by the employed and by the unemployed who were previously employed.

2.6 Social consequences

The 'self-employed' author's lack of an occupational pension extends, of course, to his widow or her widower.

The Swedish pension fund for authors pays four-sevenths of the standard pension to the widow or widower of a writer, a translator or an illustrator. In Iceland, PLR itself is paid not only to Icelandic authors but to 'their widows, widowers, or descendants who have acquired the ownership of their copyright', and the communal fund that makes awards to authors has power to make them also to the widows, widowers and descendants of dead authors.

In New Zealand the advisory committee has power to make a 'compassionate grant', in the year of the author's death only, to a dependant of an author eligible for PLR. In Australia, a dead author's PLR is paid to a surviving spouse (married or common-law) or, if the PLR committee agrees, to a surviving companion or, if it is not being paid to any of those, to 'first-generation descendants'.

In Germany, where PLR operates under copyright (creator's right), the heir to the copyright in a work is the heir to the PLR in it. Under Article 29 of the *Urheberrecht* statute of 1965, copyright 'may be conveyed pursuant to a testimentary disposition, or to co-heirs pursuant to the settlement of an estate. Otherwise, it may not be conveyed.'

Only Britain has created an independent PLR in the form of an apparently full-blown 'property right', as governments describe it, though it is subject to restrictions that do not apply to other property rights.

That it is a property right at all is not by the wish of the writers' organisations, who sought only that, should a writer die leaving a married or common-law spouse or children under the age of 18, they should continue to receive his PLR at least for a span of years. However, the Act of 1979 created the right as (under section 1, 7, a) 'transmissible by assignment or assignation, by testamentary disposition or by operation of law, as personal or moveable property'.

The copyright in an original literary work subsists (provided that the author was a 'qualified person' at the time the work was made) from the moment that the work is given a material embodiment. Copyright is not dependent on registration or any other formality. PLR, on the other hand, does not subsist unless the author has (or the co-authors have) applied on the prescribed form and the work has been accepted as eligible and registered by the Registrar. An author who is not alive to apply for registration can earn no PLR, and neither can a co-author who is alive but whose colleague is dead (cf. 1.14 and 3.7).

From registration onwards, the author may transfer the ownership of the PLR to someone else, either by will or, during his lifetime, by assignment, and any subsequent owner may transfer it similarly. However, all changes of ownership must be registered, and assignment has to be carried out on the prescribed form.

The Scheme of 1982 places limitations on the transfer of PLR. An author must, under Article 21, assign his PLR totally or not at all, in the sense that he cannot assign a portion of it while keeping another portion for himself. That provision is designed to protect authors. (See further 4.2.) There is also a limit of four on the number of persons to whom any one 'interest' (that is, in effect, the PLR in any one edition of any one title) may be assigned. That is presumably intended to limit the administrative costs that an author can impose on the fund to the detriment of his fellow-authors (since the costs are deducted before the remainder is divided up between the authors who have earned PLR), but its efficacy is doubtful, since an author might presumably assign the PLR in the hardback edition of one title to up-to-four persons and the PLR in the paperback edition of the same title to up-to-four other persons and each of the recipients might then assign his share to up-to-four yet other persons. To prevent such proliferation, the writers' organisations seek an amendment to the 1982 Scheme limiting transfers of PLR to one person. (See further 4.3.)

Once PLR has come into existence by the registration of a 'book' (that is, of an edition), it lasts, according to the 1979 Act, until 50 years after the death of the author, a provision plainly modelled on the *post auctoris mortem* duration of copyright under the British statute. Here, however, the PLR Act is holding out rather more hope to heirs – and, indeed, to people who buy or otherwise acquire ownership of an author's PLR during his lifetime – than the 1982 Scheme allows it to fulfil.

This is the result of the ruling that PLR does not subsist in a 'book' unless the author has applied for registration of that book during his lifetime, combined with the ruling that 'each new edition of a book' is to be 'treated as a separate book'.

The only works in which PLR can continue to subsist for

50 years after the author's death are, therefore, editions that were published and registered during his lifetime. On this point, too, the writers' organisations are seeking amendment. Whether an edition published in the author's lifetime continues in print after his death rests on a decision by the original publisher – and, indeed, on the original publisher's staying in business. If, as quite often happens, an author's works go out of print during his lifetime but the author is, after his death, recognised as a classic and his works are put back into print in new editions, his heirs will not, under the 1982 Scheme, receive any PLR on the new editions, no matter how frequently copies of them are borrowed from the sample libraries.

2.7 Non-PLR and pseudo-PLR

Norway and Finland operate state subsidies to authors (or, in the Norwegian case, to creators of all types) which have occasionally been mistaken for PLR.

In Norway the state allocates money under the law governing libraries, and in both Norway and Finland the amount the government allocates to subsidy of creators is a stated percentage of its annual spending on libraries.

That is, however, the only connexion between the subsidy and the libraries. Bursaries are given to authors on purely social grounds. There is no connexion between a bursary and the use made of the author's work through libraries. An author whose work is borrowed from or stocked in the libraries has no right to claim a bursary.

More insidious, because it poses as PLR but is not PLR, is the purchase-scheme. Instead of making annual payments to authors, as PLR systems do, the purchase-scheme makes a once-only payment to the author (and in some cases the publisher) when a new volume is bought by a library. The sum paid may be a flat-rate per volume or it may vary in relation to the purchase-price of the volume, but it is not related to how often the volume is borrowed or how long it stays in the library stock. Indeed, it cannot be either, since it is a payment made in advance of library use of the volume.

The purchase-scheme operates in the Netherlands, though since 1975 the Dutch writers' organisations have campaigned for the introduction in its place of genuine (loans-based) PLR.

It also operates in West Germany in a scheme devised by

the collecting society VG Wissenschaft, which in 1978 merged with VG WORT. VG Wissenschaft dealt, as its name implies, with scientific books. Since the merger of the two collecting societies, VG WORT has administered the Wissenschaft purchase-scheme in relation to scientific books, to which VG WORT allocates five-eighteenths of the sum it receives for PLR purposes, as well as administering its own spot-check-loans system (cf. 1.7) on 'belletristic' or general books, to which it allocates thirteen-eighteenths of the total.

It is left to the authors of scientific books to inform VG WORT of the purchase of their works by scientific libraries. On acceptance of his statement, the author is paid a once-only sum (consisting, in 1982, of DM 105) per title purchased. Since 1981 VG WORT has had power to make social security contributions, to a maximum of DM 100 a month, on behalf of 'self-employed' scientific writers (cf. 2.5). The Wissenschaft scheme originally made a 50 per cent payment to the publisher, but by a later agreement the publisher's fees go into a fund that finances scholarly and scientific publications with a print-run of fewer than 1,000 copies.

The purchase-scheme was suggested for introduction in Britain by a working party appointed by Lord Eccles, which reported in 1972. (See further 6.2.) It was indignation at this suggestion that prompted the formation of Writers Action Group, whose arguments for the preferability, and whose demonstrations of the feasibility, of loans-based PLR presently won the support of all writers' organisations.

The chief objections to the purchase-scheme were these. It would make no payment on future loans of volumes already in the libraries when it began (estimated at 113 million volumes) but would compel them to serve out their library life without payment to the authors. This, unfair to any author with work in the libraries, was particularly mean-spirited towards old authors, who, if they did not publish new work, would never see any payment but whose lifetime's work, amounting perhaps to scores of titles, could, under the purchase-scheme, continue to be borrowed without payment until it dropped to pieces on the shelf.

Opposition to this injustice offered by the purchase-scheme to older writers, plus opposition to the scheme's failure to meet the main social need of writers, that for an annual income (cf. 2.5), did much to unite and activate writers in Britain.

By 1974 writers in Britain were united against the purchase-scheme, but it retained the affection of some civil servants both national and local. Alongside the loans-based PLR system proposed by Writers Action Group, the purchase-scheme was tested and costed by the Technical Investigation Group, which reported in 1975 that it was no cheaper to operate than genuine PLR. Neither that nor the introduction by Act of Parliament of loans-based PLR in 1979 nor the unanimous contempt of writers for the purchase-scheme has prevented sporadic suggestions in Britain (for instance, in a letter to *The Times* of 14 September 1982) that it should be disinterred and propped up.

Part II PLR in Britain

3 The practicalities for writers and illustrators

3.1 The cardinal address

The address of the office of the Registrar of Public Lending Right is: PLR, Bayheath House, Prince Regent Street, Stockton-on-Tees, Cleveland TS18 1DF.

3.2 Issue of application forms

The Registrar, Mr John Sumsion, took up his post on 1 September 1981, but it was not until September 1982, after the completion of the PLR legislation (cf. 1.1), that his office opened to receive applications for registration.

In 1982–3 there was a mass distribution of application forms through authors' organisations, literary agencies, publishers, etc. Authors who were registered were sent further forms by the PLR office on which to apply for registration of subsequently published books.

The writer or illustrator of a published book who wants to apply but has not come into possession of an application form should send a request for one to the PLR office at the cardinal address given in 3.1.

An application form is essential because the legislation lays down that PLR does not subsist in any book unless that book has been registered by the Registrar and that registration cannot take place unless the author of the book has (or its co-authors have) applied for it on the prescribed form.

3.3 The application form

The same prescribed form serves the applications of sole authors and of co-authors. The form is sent out in the company of two leaflets. One, addressed to writers and illustrators, describes the PLR system. The other is a vital guide to filling in the application form. It gives (at the request of the writers' unions) an example of a correctly completed form.

The application form measures about 24½ by 11½ inches and is folded into a triptych. Each wing of the triptych can carry the personal particulars (described in 3.16) and the declaration (described in 3.11 and 3.13) of one applicant.

The first wing is headed 'Registration Sole Author or First Joint Author', the second 'Registration Second Joint Author' and the third 'Registration Third Joint Author'.

Thus the form can bear either the application of a sole author, who will fill in the first wing, or the applications of the up-to-three co-authors whom the 1982 Scheme recognises per 'book' (by which the Scheme means not a title but an edition). The two or three co-authors will fill in and make a declaration on one wing of the triptych apiece. (Co-authors are further discussed in 3.5 to 3.10.)

If X, Y and Z are the co-authors of a book or books, they may – indeed, they must – apply for registration of their joint work on the same application form. If X has collaborated on some books with Y and on others with Z, then all three may apply on a single form. If, however, X has also collaborated with A and Z with B, then extra forms will be needed.

The inside of the triptych is ruled with 81 lines and is designed to carry the particulars of the books (that is, the editions) of the author or the co-authors whose personal particulars are given on the outside.

The applicant is expected to enter each edition, even of the same title, on a different line. Where there are co-authors, each co-author is to be named on a different line. If a title has three co-authors and has been published in four editions, its entry will take up 12 lines.

The lines are divided into colums, whose headings bid the applicant enter the following particulars.

1 The name of the author or the names, on separate lines, of the co-authors. The name is to be given in the form it takes on the title-page. If the work is published under a pseudonym, it is the pseudonym that is to be given in the 'author's name' column on the inside of the triptych.

2 The title of the publication.

3 The percentage share a co-author is to receive. This column is relevant only when a publication has co-authors, though a sole author may enter his claim to 100 per cent of the PLR. Co-authors have to be entered on separate lines so that the right percentage will come out opposite the right

Public Lending Right

PLR

Registration
Sole Author or First Joint Author

Please complete this page in capitals either typed or in black ink.
It is suggested that you retain a copy or photocopy.

PLR Number	

Have you already applied for PLR?

For Official use only

A **Personal Details**

TITLE Delete or insert. Mr Mrs Miss

Forenames

Surname

Address

Post Code

Published Pseudonyms or other Writing Names

B **Date of Birth of author** DAY MTH YR

Is this your main or only home?
(Please mark YES or NO)

N.B. If your reply is 'NO' please explain residence on separate sheet.

C **Payment Details:** Tick here if you are willing to accept payment direct and complete the details below.

Account Number

Sorting Code — —

Bank Name and Address

Tick here if cheque payment required

Payee or Account Name

Declarations (Section D to be completed only if the author is a minor)

D I,

declare that I am the legal parent/

guardian of

named as author of the books listed overleaf.

E I,

declare the particulars contained in this form to be true, also that I satisfy the residence and personal qualifications and that the books satisfy the eligibility qualifications required by the Public Lending Right Scheme, 1982. I make this solem declaration conscientiously believing the same to be true and by virtue of the provisions of the Statutory Declarations Act, 1835.

Signed _____

Declared at _____ in the County of _____

this _____ day of _____ 19 _____ before me, _____

Please affix official stamp.

Commissioner of Oaths/Solicitor/ Justice of the Peace/Notary Public

Signed _____

PLR 7 82

69

Public Lending Right

Registration Second Joint Author

Please complete this page in capitals either typed or in black ink.

	PLR Number

Have you already applied for PLR?

1. Authors who are not applying for PLR please complete sections A and D only.
2. Eligible authors wishing to register for PLR, please complete all sections except section D.

For Official use only

A Personal Details   TITLE Delete or insert. Mr Mrs Miss

Forenames

Surname

Address

Post Code

Published Pseudonyms or other Writing Names

B Date of Birth   DAY MTH YR   Is this your main or only home? (Please mark YES or NO)   NB. If your reply is 'NO' please explain residence on separate sheet.

C Payment Details: Tick here if you are willing to accept payment direct and complete the details below.

Account Number   Sorting Code   —   —

Bank Name and Address

Tick here if cheque payment required   Payee or Account Name

Declarations

D I, declare that I am a contributor to title/s listed on this form and whilst not applying to register any right in such title/s, I give agreement to the registration of the rights set out therein.

Date _____   Signed _____

E I, declare the particulars contained in this form to be true, also that I satisfy the residence and personal qualifications and that the books satisfy the eligibility qualifications required by the Public Lending Right Scheme, 1982. I make this solemn declaration conscientiously believing the same to be true and by virtue of the provisions of the Statutory Declarations Act, 1835.

Signed _____

Declared at _____ in the County of _____

this _____ day of _____ 19_____ before me, _____

Please affix official stamp.

Commissioner of Oaths/Solicitor/ Justice of the Peace/Notary Public

Signed _____

70

Public Lending Right

Registration Third Joint Author

Please complete this page in capitals either typed or in black ink.

| | PLR Number | |

Have you already applied for PLR?

1. Authors who are not applying for PLR please complete sections A and D only.
2. Eligible authors wishing to register for PLR, please complete all sections except section D.

For Official use only

A Fersonal Details   TITLE Delete or insert.   Mr Mrs Miss

Forenames

Surname

Address

Post Code

Published Pseudonyms or other Writing Names

B Date of Birth   DAY MTH YR   Is this your main or only home? (Please mark YES or NO)   NB. If your reply is 'NO' please explain residence on separate sheet.

C Payment Details: Tick here if you are willing to accept payment direct and complete the details below.

Account Number

Sorting Code — —

Bank Name and Address

Tick here if cheque payment required

Payee or Account Name

Declarations

D I, declare that I am a contributor to title/s listed on this form and whilst not applying to register any right in such title/s, I give agreement to the registration of the rights set out therein.

Date _____   Signed _____

E I, declare the particulars contained in this form to be true, also that I satisfy the residence and personal qualifications and that the books satisfy the eligibility qualifications required by the Public Lending Right Scheme, 1982. I make this solemn declaration conscientiously believing the same to be true and by virtue of the provisions of the Statutory Declarations Act, 1835.

Signed _____

Declared at _____ in the County of _____

this _____ day of _____ 19____ before me, _____

Please affix official stamp.

Commissioner of Oaths/Solicitor/ Justice of the Peace/Notary Public

Signed _____

Book Details

Name of Author/s (as on title page)	Title of Book	% Share of PLR	Publisher	Year of Publ'n	Edn.	ISBN	For Official Use

name. Since different editions of one title count as separate books (cf. 2.6), it is open to, say, a pair of co-authors to split the PLR on, for instance, the large-print edition 50–50 and that on the paperback edition 60–40.

4 The publisher of the edition.

5 The year of publication of the edition. (This is always printed in the volume, usually on the title-page or its verso.)

6 The edition – in the sense of (a) paperback, hardback or large-print and (b) 2nd, 3rd, 4th or however the edition is described by the publisher on the verso of the title-page.

7 The ISBN (cf. 1.4). The applicant may not in all cases know the ISBN and pre-1968 publications may not have one, though some published without an ISBN have acquired one since. If an applicant cannot find the ISBNs of all his editions, the PLR office will on request, and in return for a fee to cover the cost, send him photocopies of bibliographical records, but it is not guaranteed that that will help.

3.4 Authorship

The 1982 Scheme requires (Article 4) that a person shall be treated as an author of a given book if he is either its writer or its illustrator, provided he is named on the title-page and provided that the 'nature of his contribution' to the book is *not* 'that of an editor, compiler, reviser or translator'. A book's illustrator 'includes the author of a photograph within the meaning of section 48 of the Copyright Act 1956 (a)'.

The section of the copyright Act that the Scheme refers to defines the author of a photograph as 'the person who, at the time when the photograph is taken, is the owner of the material on which it is taken'.

Because it is occasionally misunderstood, the point should be made that authorship is always assessed in relation to a particular book. There is no general ban on editors, translators, etc. The editor or translator of a particular book cannot, even if he is named on the title-page, be registered as an author of that book; but the editor or translator of one book may, of course, be the writer or illustrator of another book, and in the case of the second book he can be registered as its author or co-author and earn PLR on it.

3.5 Sole authors and co-authors

To the question 'How many authors may share the PLR earned by one title or edition?', the British PLR system replies 'Up to three writers or illustrators'. The Scheme of 1982 arbitrarily refused PLR to encyclopaedias and dictionaries if they had more than one author, but that rule was, in May 1983, cancelled (cf. 1.13). So was the rule that excluded a visual artist as such from sole authorship in PLR terms, since the same amendment order made all pages bearing print, whether the print is text or illustration, though not if it is musical score, count towards the minimum number of pages that a book must have to be eligible to earn PLR.

If the title-page of a book names more than one person but fewer than four as writers or illustrators, then all the persons named must, for purposes of PLR, be treated as co-authors of that book. Since the 1982 Scheme says that a person in this situation 'shall' (not 'may') be treated as an author of the book, this is not a matter of choice either for the Registrar or for the co-authors themselves. If there are, in the PLR sense of the word, co-authors, then the book can be registered only on the joint application of them all.

The word 'author' is colloquially used to mean 'writer', whereas in the British PLR system it means 'writer or illustrator' (and in the British copyright system means an artistic creator of any kind). It is easy for a writer, who may colloquially think of himself as 'the author' (that is, the sole author) of certain books because he is indeed the sole author of their texts, to forget that one of his titles – or perhaps only one edition of one of his titles – has been published with illustrations. If, however, he enters such a title or edition in his solo PLR application, naming only himself as author, he will be making a false statement that is covered by his declaration (see further 3.11). The PLR office checks the book details given on application forms against bibliographical records. If it detects an application by a purported sole author for registration of a title or an edition that in fact has co-authors in the sense given the word by the Scheme, then the title or edition in question will not be registered.

3.6 Co-authors

When the title-page names more than one but fewer than four writers or illustrators, the book can be registered only as a result of a joint application by them all, saying what percentage of the PLR earned by the book each is to take. In making this requirement, the Scheme of 1982 is relying on the self-interest of each to check that of the others (cf. 1.14).

The practical advice offered to co-authors by the Registrar, in his guide to completing the form and in the *Bookseller* of 5 June 1982, is that they should first get in touch to decide (a) the percentage each is to take and (b) which is to act as 'principal' and enter the particulars of the joint book or books on the application form.

The 'principal', having entered the book particulars and the percentage each co-author is to receive, should complete the first wing of the triptych in his own name and have his declaration formalised on it. He should then pass the application form to the second co-author, who should do the same on the second wing of the triptych before passing the form to the third co-author, if there is one, who should do likewise on the third wing of the triptych. The last co-author in the chain should post the application form to the PLR office (cf. 3.1).

If the first co-author is also a sole author, he may use the same application form to enter the particulars of his solo books as well as of joint books.

However, a writer might hesitate to entrust his application for work written under his sole authorship, which probably carries his main hope of PLR, to the temperament of his colleagues and the delays of the mails, including overseas mails; and in that case he may prefer to use separate application forms for sole and joint work, even though that will probably put him to the expense of an extra declaration (see 3.11).

3.7 Dead co-authors

If a book has co-authors and one of them, whether writer or illustrator, is dead, no application can be made for the book to be registered and it can never earn PLR.

The grievances caused by this provision of the 1982 Scheme are most numerous when registration has newly opened and authors are applying for registration of titles published long ago.

However, even when all such books have been discarded from the sample libraries, two types of injustice will remain so long as the 1982 Scheme remains unamended.

1 An edition whose title-page reads 'Persuasion/by Jane Austen/introduced and annotated by Z/illustrated by X', where Z and X are living, can never be registered, because the co-author Jane Austen is dead, and so Z and X can never receive any share of the PLR the edition earns.

2 The 1982 Scheme provides (under Article 6, 2, d) that a title cannot be registered before publication; and since it is normal for a year or longer to elapse between completion of the work and publication there will always be a danger that one of the co-authors will die in the interval, in which case the Scheme will deprive the survivor or survivors of PLR.

3.8 '. . . an illustrator thereof'

In ordaining that a person shall be considered a co-author of a book if he is 'an illustrator thereof', the 1982 Scheme clearly implies that the designer or executant of a visual work that is used as an illustration to a book need not be treated as a co-author of the book if, when he created the visual work, he did not know of the book's existence. A person cannot be the illustrator of a book unless he is aware of the book he is illustrating.

An historian who writes an account of the Norman Conquest which he or his publisher chooses to illustrate by reproductions of the Bayeux Tapestry should not need to fear that the creators of the Bayeux Tapestry will be treated as his co-authors and the book deprived of PLR on the grounds that his co-authors are dead. The tapestry makers cannot be properly said to be the illustrators of a text conceived some eight centuries after their death.

Likewise, if an art historian writes a book about Titian which is illustrated by reproductions of Titian's paintings, Titian cannot properly, even if the title-page should say 'with 100 reproductions of the work of Titian', be called 'the illustrator' of the book, since the book did not come into existence until four centuries after Titian had left it.

If a living critic, X, writes a book about a living painter, Z, his text may well be illustrated by reproductions of Z's oeuvre, from the watercolours he did at school in the 1930s to the grand commissions executed in the 1980s. Z's paintings, in such a case, were not conceived and executed over the years as illustrations to X's book and Z should not be considered as a co-author of the book. X is the sole author and entitled to all the PLR it may earn (just as he is to all the royalties).

It is a different matter if Z deliberately illustrates a collection of poems by A, a living poet, in which case Z and A are co-authors and must apply jointly for registration, or if Z produces illustrations to *The Tempest* which are published in a volume with the text of *The Tempest*, in which case no application for registration can be made, since Z and William Shakespeare are the co-authors, one of whom is dead.

3.9 Missing co-authors

Even when they are both or all three alive, not all co-authors can take the Registrar's advice (cf. 3.6) to get in touch with one another.

Where co-authors cannot make contact, the effect is the same as where one is dead: since there cannot be a joint application, the book cannot be registered and cannot earn PLR.

Co-authors, especially when they consist of writer and illustrator but on occasion also when they consist of a pair or a trio of writers, are not necessarily personally acquainted. It may be that the only link between them is the publisher. This link gives way if one co-author is (as illustrators often are) paid a fee instead of a royalty, because the publisher has then no need to keep a current address for him. It also gives way when the book goes out of print. Even then, copies may continue to be borrowed from the libraries, in which case the title would earn PLR were it possible for it to be registered.

3.10 Ineligible co-authors

The 1982 Scheme is more relenting when one of the co-authors is ineligible for PLR under the nationality-plus-residence rule (cf. 1.10) than it is when one of them is dead or, from the point of view of the others, missing.

Even here the Scheme insists that all the co-authors, eligible or ineligible, be alive at the time of the application and that the application be a joint one; but provided that at least one of them is eligible the application can legitimately be made.

Ineligible co-authors do not themselves receive any money from the PLR system, but they are required to give their consent, in the joint application, to the percentage to be taken by the eligible member or members of the team.

However, the Scheme provides (under Article 9, 3) that, when a book has been registered on the application of co-authors one of whom is (or two of whom are) ineligible, an ineligible co-author may, should he later become eligible, apply to receive from then on his already jointly designated percentage of the money. Presumably the Scheme believes that this gives an ineligible co-author enough self-interest in prospect to lead him to act as a curb on the greed of the eligible co-author or co-authors (cf. 1.14).

In a joint application, any co-author who is ineligible is allowed to make his part of the application, and to give his consent to the percentages in the share-out between the co-authors, on the strength simply of his signed declaration. He is excused the 'statutory declaration' (see 3.11) that the 1982 Scheme requires of authors and co-authors who stand to be paid actual money by the PLR system. On his (second or third) triptych wing of the application form an ineligible co-author is required only to complete and sign Declaration D, 'I, ————————————————, declare that I am a contributor to title/s listed on this form and whilst not applying to register any right in such title/s I give agreement to the registration of the rights set out therein'.

Since an ineligible co-author may well be ineligible by virtue of residing outside the United Kingdom, this handily also excuses the British government from stating what it would accept as an overseas version of a 'statutory declaration'.

3.11 The statutory declaration

Whereas New Zealand charges a small fee (in 1976, $5) when an author first applies for PLR but makes no charge when he adds further titles to his list, the British PLR Scheme of 1982 includes a device that is fairly certain to impose recurrent charges on authors, to the financial benefit not of the PLR fund or of the government but of the legal profession.

Any applicant for registration who, unlike an ineligible co-author (cf. 3.10), stands to earn money himself from the PLR system is required to provide with his application a 'statutory declaration' or 'a declaration before a Notary Public'.

The declaration is printed, as Declaration E, on each triptych wing of the application form: 'I————————————, declare the particulars contained in this form to be true, also that I satisfy the residence and personal qualifications and that the books satisfy the eligibility qualifications required by the Public Lending Right Scheme, 1982. I make this solemn declaration conscientiously believing the same to be true and by virtue of the provisions of the Statutory Declarations Act, 1835.'

This the applicant is required to sign in the presence of a commissioner of oaths, a solicitor, a Justice of the Peace or a notary public, who is required to place his official rubber stamp on it.

The application form names the four acceptable professions but does not state that a Justice of the Peace performs the service free whereas the other three make a charge (£2 in 1982), though that was stated in a government answer in November 1982 to a question in the House of Lords put by Lord Vaizey (a member, while it existed, of Writers Action Group), which also said that the requirement of a statutory declaration was 'considered desirable. . . in order to reduce the risk of false declarations'.

While the Scheme was being drafted by the Office of Arts and Libraries (cf. 1.13), the writers' organisations put forward the view that there was sufficient safeguard in the 1979 Act, which, under section 4, 7, provides for a fine of up to £1,000 on anyone who knowingly or recklessly makes a statement that is false in a material particular.

The writers were, however, over-ruled and the 1982 Scheme introduced the requirement for a statutory declaration. It is possible that the statutory declaration is considered to be a protection for the Registrar, since, in accepting that the applicant is the author of the books concerned and that he and they are eligible by the rules of the Scheme, the Registrar is (under Article 18) 'entitled to rely upon a statutory declaration or a declaration made before a Notary Public'. It is difficult, however, to understand why the Scheme could not have made him entitled to rely on a simple signed declaration, especially one urged towards truthfulness by the threat of a fine.

The requirement that they visit a lawyer and go through an unfamiliar formal procedure is liable to deter authors from applying, especially if they are disabled or live in a remote place.

An applicant unable to find a Justice of the Peace is further deterred by the cost, which he has to undertake before knowing (indeed, in order to find out) whether the work for whose registration he is applying will earn enough PLR to repay his £2 investment by surpassing the £5 bottom limit (cf. 1.17), below which no payment is made.

The cost falls particularly heavily in the first place on writers and illustrators (of, for instance, children's books) who enter fresh co-authorship combinations with each fresh title, since one application form can accommodate only three co-authors and each has to make his statutory declaration.

There is also, for all practising authors, a recurrent cost, since the registration of every new title and every new edition (even an edition of a title already registered) requires a new statutory declaration. An author who holds back from registering, say, the hardback edition of a title until the paperback and the large-print editions have been published as well, so that he can apply for registration of them all on one form and under one statutory declaration, will forfeit the PLR the hardback might have earned during the interval.

3.12 Under-age authors

The Scheme of 1982 makes provision for the work of an author who 'is not of full age' (which in 1982 meant one who is younger than 18) to be registered in the name of his parent or guardian (Article 17, 3) and for the registration to be transferred to the author himself if he applies to the Registrar when he attains full age (Article 25). If he omits to apply, the PLR will continue to be paid to the parent or guardian.

The first triptych wing of the application form gives, as Declaration D, the wording of the statutory declaration to be made, in his own name, by the parent or guardian. The other two wings lack this. The PLR office would presumably have to issue a new version of the form should an application be mooted for registration of a work by three co-authors all under 18.

3.13 Effects of the statutory declaration

The practical effects of the requirement for a formalised declaration are to deter some authors and to oblige some of those who overcome the deterrence to gamble on whether the cost of making an application will be overtaken by the results.

Morally, the effect is to transfer responsibility for keeping the rules of the PLR system from the bureaucracy to the applicant. This effect is made by the wording of the declaration, not by its formality. The effect would be the same if a simple signed declaration in the same words were acceptable.

As he would expect to be, the applicant is required to vouch for the truth of the particulars he enters on his application form about matters where he can be considered the best informed person. He is also, however, required to vouch for the conformity of the titles he has entered, and of himself as their author, to the rules of the PLR system as set out in the 1982 Scheme.

This obliges him to master the rules and to check each item in his application for conformity with them. It also obliges him to grasp that the rules forbid him to apply on his own for registration of any title or edition that has, in the sense given the word by the rules in the Scheme, a co-author (cf. 3.5) and that, if he does, he will have made a false statement in his declaration.

3.14 Eligible persons

It is strange that the statutory declaration does not include an explicit affirmation by the applicant that he is the author or an author of the books for whose registration he is applying.

However, the first qualification the Scheme lays down (in Article 5, 1) for an 'eligible person' is that he be an author of the book in question within the meaning the Scheme gives the word 'author' (cf. 3.4). Presumably, therefore, in a roundabout way, when the applicant declares 'I satisfy the residence and personal qualifications' required by the 1982 Scheme, the 'personal' qualifications include the fact that he is the author of the books he has entered on the form. Presumably the 'personal' qualifications also tacitly include the nationality qualification. On forms printed since spring 1983, the declaration explicitly mentions 'citizenship' but omits 'personal' requirements, thus leaving authorship unvouched for.

The nationality-plus-residence criterion (cf. 1.10) is set out in full in Article 5 of the 1982 Scheme. An author is eligible if he 'is a British citizen or. . . is a national of the United Kingdom or of any other member state of the European Economic Community' and if, at the time of his application, he also 'has his only or principal home in the United Kingdom, or, if he has no home, has been present in the United Kingdom for not less than twelve months out of the preceding twenty-four months'.

The Article adds the explanation that, if the author has more than one home, then his 'principal' home is the one where 'he has been for the longest aggregate period during the twenty-four months immediately preceding his application'.

What the Scheme requires is that the applicant should meet the residence-plus-nationality criterion at the time he makes his application. Provided he does so, he can apply for registration of works created and published at a time when he was not an EEC citizen and/or was not resident in the UK. Similarly, once a title has been registered, the author can continue to draw any PLR it earns even if he ceases to be an EEC citizen and/or a resident of the UK. In that case, however, he will not be able to apply for registration of titles published after he ceased to fulfil the requirements.

An expatriate author of a largeish and much-borrowed oeuvre might consider it worth his while, provided he has retained the necessary EEC nationality, to establish UK residence for long enough to make registration of his oeuvre to date possible, though he would have to bear in mind that, once he has again abandoned UK residence, he cannot apply for registration of further titles and that the most he can earn in PLR per year is £5,000 (cf. 1.17).

3.15 Eligible books

Applicants are required to declare that the books they enter on their application forms meet the criteria of eligibility laid down by the 1982 Scheme.

The criteria are set out in Article 6, which also requires 'each volume of a work published in two or more volumes' and 'each new edition of a book' to be treated as 'a separate book'. This obliges the applicant to make a separate entry on his form for each edition of a title and for each volume of a multi-volume work.

To make sure that each edition he lists is eligible demands some mental agility on the applicant's part.

To be eligible, an edition *must not* (A) bear, in the place of the name of 'an author who is a natural person', the name of 'a body corporate or an unincorporated association', (B) be in Crown copyright, (C) have more than three authors in the sense meant by the Scheme (cf. 3.4), (D) be 'wholly or mainly a musical score' (an addition made in May 1983) or (E) be a serial publication; and it *must* (a) have an eligible author or co-author named on the title-page, (b) be printed and bound (paperbacks counting as bound), (c) have been offered for sale to the public and (d) meet the minimum page requirement.

Of these, item (c) requires both that the work should not be a free handout and that it should have been published before application is made for its registration. Writers, who are accustomed to being asked by *Who's Who* and similar compilations to enter their forthcoming titles in advance, have to remind themselves that the PLR rules take the opposite line, even though the spacing out of applications creates the need for extra statutory declarations (cf. 3.11) and increases the risk of a co-author's dying before registration and rendering registration impossible (cf. 3.7).

Item (d) requires that a copy of an eligible title or edition shall contain a minimum of 32 pages or 24 pages in cases where at least half are pages of poetry or drama. The irrationality of this requirement, given that pages are not of standard size and do not contain a standard number of words, is argued in 1.15.

The Scheme of 1982 specifically excluded endpapers from the pages that count towards the necessary minimum and decreed that, if a page was to count towards the minimum, at least half its area, margin excluded, must be 'occupied by print otherwise than by way of a printed illustration'. Even apart from the fact that many authors proved not to know what endpapers were (folded sheets at the beginning and the end of a volume, half the folded sheet being stuck to the inside of the cover, the other half usually remaining free-moving like a page), these rules caused practical difficulties when registration began in 1982. An author in difficulty about mustering the necessary minimum number of pages might hesitate over a page on which text and illustrations were interspersed and no regular margin was defined, in which case the best advice the Registrar could offer him was to put a transparent grid over the doubtful page and count how many squares were occupied by text and how many by illustration. By May 1983 these problems had prompted the minister for the arts to abolish the requirement that at least half the page area be occupied by text and substitute the rule under which all pages, endpapers included, that carry print count towards the requisite minimum number of pages (cf. 1.13).

3.16 Personal particulars

In his statutory declaration the applicant vouches for the truth of the particulars given in his application. His personal particulars are elicited from him when he fills in blanks and boxes on his wing of the triptych. The information he gives in this way consists of: (a) his forenames, surname and title and his address; (b) his 'published pseudonyms or other writing names'; (c) the day, month and year of his birth; (d) a 'Yes' or 'No' answer to 'Is this your main or only home?'; and (e) the method by which he chooses to be paid any PLR he earns.

Item (a). The name the applicant is required to give is that which represents his 'true identity'.

Married women who write or illustrate books under their maiden name (of whom there are many, for the simple reason that many of them began publishing before marriage and after it stuck to the name they had already established) are obliged to make their PLR applications in their married name. Authors of either sex who are known in everyday life, as well as on their books, by a pseudonym are obliged to apply in the name shown on their birth certificate or, if they are married and female, on their marriage certificate.

Authors are registered for PLR not under the name in which they practise authorship but under that of their 'true identity'. This is required by Article 8, a, iii of the 1982 Scheme, which obliges the register to record 'the true identity' of an author if that differs from the name given on the title-page of the book registered.

This requirement was contested by the writers' organisations during the drafting of the Scheme.

It is, of course, necessary for the applicant to list all his pseudonyms, as he is indeed asked to do under item (b), so that the top limit of £5,000 in a year may be applied to the total PLR earnings of one person (cf. 1.17). There is, however, no technical reason why the PLR system needs his 'true identity', a concept of, in any case, doubtful validity in Britain. Professional names may be adopted for good cause (which, however, the PLR system has no occasion to enquire into). They may serve the writer in ordinary as well as professional life, in which case they might claim to represent his truest, in the sense of most widely recognised, identity. Authors sign contracts with their publishers in their professional names and no one queries their authenticity. Moreover, since the Act of 1979 confers PLR on 'authors', it can be argued that they should be entitled to be registered for it in the name in which they practise authorship.

The writers' organisations were over-ruled by the Office of Arts and Libraries and the 'true identity' requirement went into the 1982 Scheme.

Authors anxious to conceal their non-professional names from household or neighbours should be warned that when the PLR office communicates with a registered author it addresses the envelope to him under his 'true identity'.

Item (c). Nothing in the PLR Act or Scheme makes registration conditional on the applicant's disclosing the date of his birth. The PLR office asks for the information in the belief that it may help sort out identities in cases where authors have the same or confusingly similar names.

Item (d). In the question 'Is this your main or only home?', the 'this' presumably refers to the address the applicant has given five lines above. The question is presumably designed to elicit whether the applicant meets the residence qualification (cf. 3.14) by having his 'only or principal home' in the United Kingdom.

If the applicant's answer to the question is 'No', the application form asks him to 'explain residence on separate sheet'. An applicant whose answer is 'No' may still be qualified if the explanation he gives on a separate sheet is either that he has no home but has spent at least 12 of the past 24 months in the UK or that he has several homes which include one in the UK which is the one where he has spent the longest accumulated total of time in the course of the past 24 months.

The application form includes no query, just as the statutory declaration originally included no statement, on the subject of nationality (cf. 3.14). It is left to the applicant to remember that he must qualify on this count before he fills in his form, gets it sworn and sends it to the PLR office.

3.17 After the application

After despatching his completed and formally witnessed form, the applicant receives a letter of acknowledgement. Provided that the PLR office has not discovered any discrepancy that would affect eligibility between the particulars given in the application and the bibliographical records, the applicant is then sent confirmation of the registration of his titles, in the form of a computer print-out, on green and white lines, of his entry in the register.

The print-out informs him of his author registration number, which he is expected to cite in future applications for the registration of further titles and in correspondence with the PLR office.

As a rule the print-out lists, perhaps abbreviated into computerese, the particulars about each edition that the applicant entered on the inside of his application form (cf. 3.3), with a line of print-out allotted to each edition. When, however, the applicant has listed pre-ISBN editions, they may all appear on one line of the print-out, with publisher and publication date omitted, under the summary 'No ISBN found', in which case the PLR office usually appends an assurance that they have all been registered for PLR.

Together with his print-out, the now registered author receives tear-off forms (a) acknowledging receipt of the print-out and (b) laying formal claim to payment of any PLR earned. These he is required to sign and return to the PLR office, which cannot pay him his PLR unless he does.

If the PLR office has been able to add to the ISBNs listed in the application, they appear asterisked on the print-out and the author is asked to send confirmation to the PLR office that he wants them to stand in his entry on the register.

The author is also sent an amendment form. On this he may enter and send at any time to the PLR office changes to his entry on the register of a kind that do not affect his eligibility, such as changes of name or address and newly-discovered ISBNs of titles that have already been registered without them.

3.18 Claim, renunciation, etc.

The reason that an author whose work has been registered is required to submit a separate claim to be paid his PLR lies in the 1979 Act. In section 1, 7 the Act requires the Scheme to make provision for PLR 'to be established by registration' (which itself depends, under section 4, 4, on application) and also 'to be claimed by or on behalf of the person for the time being entitled'. The Scheme was obliged to obey the Act, and the PLR office to obey the Scheme, in literal fashion.

The Act gives the impression of having been written in the belief that authors needed protection from having PLR thrust on them against their will.

In practice, an author who does not want any PLR his work may earn can simply abstain from applying. It is unlikely that an author could complete an application form, get it statutorily witnessed and send it to Stockton-on-Tees without noticing what he was doing or intending to do it. Should that happen, he will still not have his PLR forced upon him. He need only abstain from signing and posting his claim form.

Not satisfied with requiring all these voluntary acts by an author before he comes into any danger of being paid PLR, the Act further requires the Scheme to provide for PLR 'to be renounced (either in whole or in part, and either temporarily or for all time) on notice being given to the Registrar to that effect'.

The Scheme duly makes provision for the renunciation of PLR in Article 32 and Schedule 1, Part III.

The PLR on a given book can be renounced only after the registration of that book has been applied for and accomplished. A registered owner, including an heir or a person to whom the PLR has been assigned (cf. 2.6), who wants to renounce must seek from the Registrar (cf. 3.1) the appropriate form. The Scheme rules that an 'application for renunciation shall bear the proper Inland Revenue stamp impressed thereon'.

4 Reflections for writers and illustrators

4.1 Points to watch

The rules in the 1982 Scheme fell, sometimes in defiance of the advice of the writers' organisations, on existing titles and cut some of them out of the PLR system. Where, however, a work is still in the writing or illustrating or where a publishing contract for it is still in negotiation, it may be that a smallish action by the writer or illustrator or by his agent can make sure that, when the work reaches publication, it will be eligible for registration for PLR. So long as the relevant items in the 1982 Scheme remain unamended, some points will remain worth keeping an eye on. Indeed, the Scheme may unintentionally prompt some small changes in publishing and contracting practice.

1 An author cannot apply for registration of a title unless his name is on the title-page. It is unlikely, though not impossible, that the name of a sole writer would be omitted, but even sole writers where there is any doubt and certainly co-authors, especially illustrators, would be wise to make absolutely sure through the publishing contract that their names will appear on the title-page.

2 When the text is short, a writer would be wise to seek a contractual undertaking that the publisher will produce the volume in a format that meets all the current minimum page requirements for PLR (cf. 3.15).

3 When a co-authorship team is chosen by the publisher rather than the authors themselves, they would be well-advised to insist on being put in touch immediately and to take care to remain in touch until publication and registration are accomplished (cf. 3.9).

4 Cold-eyed co-authors will assess one another as potential bad risks for survival until publication and registration (cf. 3.7) and also, since the rule that co-authors must make a joint application gives each veto powers over the others, as potential bad risks in terms of laziness or vindictiveness (cf. 3.5).

5 Anyone asked by a publisher to write an introduction or commentary for a new edition of a work by an author now dead should bear in mind that such an edition will not be

eligible for PLR (cf. 3.7).

The rule that a joint work cannot be registered for PLR if any of the co-authors is dead is one that the writers' organisations were in 1983 trying to dislodge (see further 4.4). Should it remain in force despite them, writers might be moved to try to introduce a new fashion for two-volume publication. If the text by the dead author occupied one volume and the commentary by the living author another, then the rule that each volume of a two-volume work must be treated as a separate book (cf. 3.15) would ensure that the living writer could apply for and receive registration.

If one-volume publication is unavoidable, the writer of the commentary (and likewise an illustrator commissioned to illustrate the work of a dead author) should at least be able to make sure that his payment compensates him for the forfeiture of his PLR.

6 By lifting (cf. 1.13) the PLR embargo on an encyclopaedia, dictionary or 'comparable publication', the minister for the arts made it unnecessary for teams of co-authors to seek methods of wriggling round it, whether by re-casting the material in non-alphabetical order, thereby making the book essentially not 'comparable' with an encyclopaedia or dictionary, or by calling the book 'an all-round education' and hoping it would pass unnoticed that that is a rough translation of 'encyclopaedia'.

4.2 Publishers and PLR

While the PLR Bill was going through Parliament, the minister responsible (Lord Donaldson of Kingsbridge, minister for the arts at the time) made this statement in the House of Lords: 'I am sure that the publishers will recognise, along with everyone else, that the Public Lending Right is being established at public expense for the benefit of authors alone.'

Most publishers did recognise it. Between 1952 and 1972 there were divergent speculations in Britain about the form PLR legislation would take and the source of PLR funds, and some of the speculations included a share for publishers. However, Writers Action Group, formed in 1972, contained a small group of publisher associate members who both renounced and denounced a share for publishers. Speculation was ended by the introduction in 1976 of a government PLR Bill conferring PLR on authors and funding it from central public funds, with the consequences described by Lord Donaldson. After the passage of the Act only a scattering of publishers defied what Lord Willis (in a letter to *The Times* of 1 May 1982) described as 'the clear wish of Parliament that PLR should benefit authors and authors alone'.

However, an article by Robert Hewison in the *Times Literary Supplement* of 16 April 1982 gave warning of publisher–author contracts 'already in operation' under which the publisher purported to take a percentage of any PLR earned by the author on the book. The Publishers Association suggested that it was legitimate for publishers to negotiate such clauses in contracts and that it was not only legitimate but possible for the publisher to act on the author's behalf in relation to the PLR office and then take his cut.

That misapprehension should have been quashed by a reading of the 1982 Scheme. In fact, application for registration can be made only by the author or the co-authors of the book concerned. Once the right has been registered, the author can assign it to up-to-four people, but he cannot assign a percentage of it to another person while keeping a percentage for himself (cf. 2.6 and Scheme, Article 21).

These rules give considerable protection to any authors who, lacking an agent and a union to protect them, might be pressed to sign contracts giving a percentage of the PLR to the publisher. At the least, the PLR rules would make it extremely difficult for the publisher to enforce any such claim.

4.3 Reforms sought

By early 1983 the writers' unions were seeking in unison to convince the government of the need for the following reforms in the PLR system.

Under the 1979 Act (section 2,3), the first change listed here could, given Treasury approval, be introduced by statutory instrument and then approved by resolution of the House of Commons. All the others would require parliamentary amendment of the Scheme of 1982. The two reforms itemised here under 11 would need amendment both of the 1982 Scheme and of the 1979 Act, and so might the reform listed as item 9.

1 The total PLR fund, whose rate of £2 million a year was

fixed in 1979 (that is, five years before any payments were made to authors) should be seriously increased.

2 British PLR should depend on a residence criterion alone and should be made reciprocal with the PLR system in any country that pays PLR to British authors (cf. 1.10 – 1.12).

3 Translators (cf. 3.4) should be made eligible for a (fixed) share of PLR.

4 Where a co-author is dead or untraceable by his co-author(s), a co-author of the book who is alive and prepared to sign a statement to the effect that one of his co-authors is dead or untraceable should be able to apply for registration. He should receive (a) half or one third of the PLR earned by the book (according to the number of the co-authors) in cases where the contributions of the co-authors are undifferentiated or (b) in cases where the contributions are distinct (for instance, the contributions of one writer and one illustrator), a percentage of the PLR proportionate to the ratio between the number of pages to which he has made any contribution and the total number when multi-author pages are counted twice (cf. 3.7, 3.9 and 3.10).

5 The requirement for a statutory declaration (cf. 3.11) should be abolished; all statements, including the one suggested in item 4 above, should need only a signature, since the penalty threatened under the 1979 Act is sufficient deterrent to false statements.

6 An encyclopaedia or dictionary should be eligible for PLR with up-to-three co-authors. The minister for the arts introduced this reform in May 1983 (cf. 1.13).

7 The minimum page count (cf.1.15 and 3.15) should be abolished. Any printed, bound and published work that a library thinks worth stocking and borrowers think worth taking out should be eligible for PLR. The reform introduced by the minister for the arts in May 1983 (cf. 1.13) modified only the conditions under which a page counts as a page towards the minimum number. It does not remove the requirement of a minimum number of pages.

8 Where there is no change of authorship (by, that is, the addition or subtraction of a co-author such as an illustrator) between one edition of a title and another, all editions of a title should be treated as one book, which would allow heirs to benefit from posthumous editions and thus in practice to enjoy the promised posthumous duration of PLR (cf. 2.6).

9 The bottom limit on payment should be applied per

author instead of per edition (cf. 1.17 and 5.11). The minister for the arts was expected to introduce in the autumn of 1983 an amendment to the Scheme that would lower the sum named as the bottom limit. On the subject of applying the limits per edition or per author, the Office of Arts and Libraries takes the view that the 1979 Act gives the Scheme authority to apply the upper limit per author but binds it to apply the lower limit per edition. If that interpretation of the Act is correct, a reform that applied the lower limit per author instead of per edition would require amendment of the 1979 Act as well as of the 1982 Scheme.

10 The number of people to whom the owner of the PLR in a book may assign or bequeath it should be reduced from four to one (cf. 2.6).

11 Active and practical plans should be made (a) to introduce, parallel with the payments on loans of lending volumes, the Swedish method of paying on volumes held on library premises for reference (cf. 1.8) and (b) to extend the loans sample to libraries of other types than public libraries (cf. 1.9) and to increase the total fund sufficiently to cover payment for the full range of library loans in Britain.

4.4 The other cardinal address

Although it was unlikely to be taken as a model of 'correct' usage in forms of address (a writer called Sir Toby Belch being liable to receive from it a letter beginning 'Dear Sir Belch'), the PLR office had by 1983 won the reputation with authors of sending friendly answers to their queries and doing its best to guide them through the complexity of the system.

Authors should, however, bear in mind that the express duty of the Registrar is to act, and act literally, on the rules of the PLR Scheme approved by Parliament. An author who is in doubt about the rules or their application to his own work can expect from the PLR office a sympathetic and helpful reply to his questions; but if the author's true purpose is not to enquire about but to object to the rules, he would be wise to remember that the PLR office did not make them and has no power to change them to suit his case, no matter how reasonable his arguments may be. An author's opinion about the rules might more pertinently be addressed to: The Minister for the Arts, Office of Arts and Libraries, Department of Education and

Science, Elizabeth House, York Road, London SE1 7PH.

5 Administration

5.1 The PLR Year

The PLR year runs from 1 July to 30 June. (The only exception is described in 5.2 below.)

During those 12 months a complete loans record is taken in the 16 sample libraries (cf. 1.7).

As soon as Year 1's loans record is complete, the loans record begins to be taken for Year 2, in a sample of libraries now modified by 'rotation' (cf. 1.7). On 30 June in Year 1, four libraries are dropped from the sample and on 1 July in Year 2 four fresh libraries are taken into it.

The loans record of Year 1 and the entries made or remaining on the register during Year 1 are collated by the PLR office during the first six months (July to December) of Year 2. The payments thus calculated to be due to registered authors in respect of Year 1 are made in the eighth month (February) of Year 2.

5.2 Exception

During the PLR system's first year and a half of operation, the normal PLR cycle described above was dislocated.

This was the result of the delay in drafting the Scheme and presenting it for parliamentary approval, which had to be accomplished before the system had authority to go into action (cf. 1.2 and 1.13).

In order to keep to the schedule of making the first payments to authors in February 1984, those payments had to be calculated by collating a register compiled over nine months (1 September 1982 to 30 June 1983) with a loans record taken, in the initial sample of libraries, over the course of only six months (1 January to 30 June 1983). The number of loans ascribed in the record to each registered edition was to be doubled in order to give a representation of a full year's loans.

Having yielded the first loans record in this way, the initial sample of 16 libraries (see 5.4) was due to continue in existence, without rotation, until 30 June 1984, accumulating a further loans record, this time covering 12 months, to be used as the basis of the second batch of payments to authors.

5.3 The libraries

In any given PLR year, only 16 public-library service points (cf. 2.4) take part in the PLR operation. These 16 sample libraries are designated by the Registrar within a framework laid down by the Scheme (in Article 38 and Schedule 2). The framework combines criteria of geography, local government organisation and the size of service points.

Each library in the sample is required to send the PLR office every month a magnetic tape that records all the book loans it has made. Distinguishing, on the tape, between loans of registered books and loans of books which have not been registered and therefore earn no PLR is the task of the PLR office, not of the libraries.

The expenditure a sample library undertakes in the course of playing its part in the PLR system is repaid to the local library authority concerned by the PLR office on an actual cost basis whose terms are set out in Articles 43 and 44 of the 1982 Scheme.

So far as possible within the Scheme's geographical requirements, the libraries designated for the sample are libraries already using a computerised system for book issues (cf. 1.7). Reimbursement to the local authorities includes the cost of any modifications the libraries make for PLR purposes to their computer programs.

The Registrar wrote in the *Library Association Record*, July/August 1982: 'It is no exaggeration to say that in many cases participation in PLR under this system will not only be unnoticed by the public – but will hardly be noticed by library staff.'

5.4 Initial sample

In March 1982 the Registrar designated the 16 libraries that constituted the initial sample (cf. 5.2), which began to take the loans record on 1 January 1983.

The libraries in the initial sample were named as:-
Allestree; Buxton; Darlington; Bournemouth (Kinson); Dartford; Witham; Formby; Gateshead; Beckenham;

Hendon; Carmarthen; Wrexham; Glasgow (Hillhead); Glasgow (Pollock); Belfast Central; Belfast, Ormeau Road.

The concentration of the initial sample on libraries already computerised results, in some cases, in the representation of a whole region (Scotland, Northern Ireland) by two libraries in the same city.

5.5 Constituents of the sample

The 16 service points in the sample comprise ten 'principal' service points and six 'ordinary' ones. These are the two sizes of service point defined in Article 36 of the 1982 Scheme. A 'principal' service point either makes more than 500,000 book issues a year or is the largest (or nearly the largest) in its local authority area. An 'ordinary' service point is simply one making fewer than 500,000 issues.

The geographical distribution of service points within seven groups of local library authority areas is described in Article 38, 1 and Schedule 2 of the 1982 Scheme.

From the initial sample the PLR office expected to receive a total accumulated record of between six and seven million issues a year, which would represent something between 1.2 per cent and 1.07 per cent, dependent partly on the totals used (see further 5.11), of all public-library issues in Britain.

5.6 PLR computer

In 1982 the PLR office acquired a Perkin-Elmer 3210 mini-computer with two 300 megabyte disks and eight visual display units, the system to be online but not to involve real-time operation.

Programming was done under contract by Logica, the computer consultants who pioneered PLR techniques in Britain by virtue of the advice they (literally) gave to Writers Action Group in the course of WAG's campaign from 1972 onwards to persuade the government that computerised loans sampling was feasible (cf. 1.7 and 6.3).

5.7 PLR computer files

The central business of the PLR computer is to hold and eventually compare two files: I the file of registered authors and the registered editions of their works and II the file showing the number of loans made by the sample libraries of each registered edition.

File I accumulates as applications come in from authors for the registration of editions and File II as the loans-record tapes come in from the sample libraries and the loans of registered works are picked out.

By comparing the two files the computer arrives at the year's total of loans for each registered edition and can calculate the sum due to each author.

For such comparison to be possible it is essential that a given title in a given edition be identified by the same number in both files, and both files indeed use the identifying numbers recognised by the PLR office (see further 5.8).

The difficulty in building the files consists in the fact that the two outside sources of information on which they rely, namely authors' applications and the loans records from the sample libraries, may not give the identifying number in the code required by the PLR system.

To resolve the difficulty, the PLR computer carries two further types of file: III a bibliographical database consisting of the appropriate records from LASER (London and South East Regional Lending Co-operative), plus any otherwise unidentified editions found in authors' applications or in the loans records from the sample libraries, and IV a link file in respect of each sample library that can translate the identifying code number used in that sample library's loans record into the identifying code for the same title and edition used by the PLR Files I and II.

5.8 ISBNs and other codes used by PLR

The preference of the PLR office is to identify a given title in a given edition by means of the ISBN (cf. 1.4). Where a work has been numbered according to several codes, priority goes to the ISBN (International Standard Book Number).

The ISBN system in the United Kingdom is administered by the Standard Book Numbering Agency, which is a subsidiary company of J. Whitaker & Sons, Limited, publishers of the *Bookseller* and *British Books in Print*.

The digits that make each ISBN unique to a particular title (in a particular edition) consist of (in this order, from left to right):- (a) an initial digit or group signifying the language of the publication (for instance, 3 signifies the German language and 0 the English language, irrespective of the place of publication); (b) a three-digit number signifying the publisher, which remains constant to that publisher and is assigned to him by the Standard Book Numbering Agency; (c) a series of digits which is allotted, usually in the form of a number in a sequence, by the publisher to the edition he is publishing; and (d) a check digit that enables automated systems to check on the correctitude of the earlier components.

The system was instituted in 1968, and in 1970 publishers retrospectively allocated ISBNs to those of their pre-1968 publications that were then still in print.

However, both the applications from authors for PLR registration and the loans records of the sample libraries are liable to lack some ISBNs. The author or the library catalogue may have failed to find the ISBN or to catch up with a retrospectively issued ISBN; or there may be no ISBN. In addition, the ISBN (which is not always correctly printed in the volume itself) may be wrongly recorded in the library catalogue. A sample library that uses ISBNs to identify the titles loaned usually derives the ISBN from its (probably computerised) catalogue rather than from the volume itself. For PLR purposes there is a further difficulty, therefore, in the fact that not all libraries include their paperback holdings in their computerised catalogues.

In these cases the first task of the PLR office is to correct the erroneous and to supply the missing ISBNs through its bibliographical records.

There remains, however, a core (estimated in 1982 at 12 to 15 per cent of the titles in question) of editions registered and editions lent by the sample libraries for which no ISBN can be found.

In these core cases the PLR office identifies the work by a number belonging to a different code system. This may be the British National Bibliography (BNB) number; or a LASER 'ff' number, which is a number adopted by libraries that are members of LASER (cf. 5.7) in place of the ISBN or the BNB number; or a pseudo-ISBN (cf. 1.4), a unique number employing the principles of the ISBN code, which is assigned to the title in the edition in question by the Registrar's office, for use in connexion with PLR alone, and which is prefixed 0555.

5.9 Identifiers required from sample libraries

In any given sample of libraries it can be expected that some will conduct their own book-issuing business in terms of ISBNs, though even so there will be cases where the ISBN is unknown or non-existent, and other libraries will use a code of their own, which usually consists of numbers assigned in sequence to the volumes in the library: accession numbers, issued in sequence by the library to the volumes as they join the collection, or the numbers given under one of the commercial systems for automating library routines.

Where a sample library uses a code of its own, the PLR office terms it a 'local book code'.

The PLR Act of 1979 gives the Scheme power to provide for the Registrar to require local library authorities to give loans information 'as and when, and in the form in which, the Registrar may call for it' (section 3, 5, a).

In practice, the Registrar requires the sample libraries to supply the loans record in different form according to whether the library uses the ISBN code or its own 'local book code'.

1 Libraries using ISBNs are required to record the loans they make with an identification of the work lent that consists of the ISBN, the library copy number and a 'short contributor name' embodying the first four letters of the surname of the author (or of the principal contributor where there is more than one). Besides giving the library copy number, which is obligatory, the library may opt to add the number of copies which the library holds of the edition in question.

The 'short contributor name' makes it easier for the PLR office to collate the library loan with the PLR file of registered authors and editions and to cross-check that the ISBN is correct.

Where, however, a sample library using the ISBN code cannot in fact supply the ISBN of a work it has lent out, the loans record is required to give fuller identification, including the title, the 'local book code' number and the full name of the author or of the contributors. It is optional for the library to add the name of the publisher and the year of publication.

2 A sample library that uses a 'local book code' is required to give fuller information than sample libraries using ISBNs. Indeed, a 'local book code' library is required to give both the 'local' number and the ISBN, as well as the 'short contributor name'. In cases where a 'local book code' library cannot find the ISBN, it is required to give the 'local book code' number, the local title number, the title and the full name of the author or of the contributors, with the option to add the number of copies held in the library, the publisher and the year of publication.

5.10 Precaution

In totalling the number of loans attributed by the loans records from the sample libraries to each registered edition, the PLR computer is programmed to draw attention to cases where a given copy of a title is loaned from one library more than 12 times in a month.

That is a precaution against attempts by an author or the acolyte of an author to push the author's loans in the sample (and therefore the author's earnings from PLR) to artificial heights.

Presumably the PLR office investigates instances in case there should be a legitimate cause, but the 1982 Scheme requires (under Article 42, 3) that 'any loans of a copy of a book at a particular sampling point in excess of twelve within a month shall be disregarded'. It would therefore be illegal for the excess loans to be paid for.

5.11 Totals, grossing up, payment

The loans attributed to each registered edition in the loans records from the sample libraries are totalled. The result is grossed up in relation to the total number of loans made, according to CIPFA (Chartered Institute of Public Finance and Accountancy) figures, in the course of a year, from public libraries in the regional group to which the sample library belongs. The seven regional groups are named in Schedule 2 of the 1982 Scheme. The Scheme does not specify the source of the annual total of loans made in a region that is to be used in grossing up but only (under Article 42) that they be totals 'during the financial year ending in the sampling year' or, if those are not available, the most recent that are.

Unlike those in the Municipal Year Book (cf. 2.4), the loans published by CIPFA are given in round figures (thousands). Loans figures are published only for England, Wales, Scotland and Northern Ireland, not for each library authority. If an authority fails to make a return, its loans are omitted from the total of loans ascribed to the country concerned.

The grossed up figures from the seven regional groups are then totalled to produce an overall loans figure (a) per registered edition and (b) per registered author.

Payment is then calculated within (a) the bottom limit (fixed in 1982 at £5 but likely to be lowered in autumn 1983), which applies per edition, and (b) the top limit of £5,000, which applies per author (cf. 1.17 and 4.3). In the application of the top limit the sums earned by all the works originally registered in the name of a given author (and published under all his pseudonyms) are added together, even if he has assigned (cf. 2.6) the PLR in some or all of them to other people (1982 Scheme, Article 46, 2, b).

The formulae by which payment is calculated in relation to grossed up loans are laid down in Article 46 of the Scheme, which names a fee per loan of half a penny (0.5 p).

That sum is in effect an estimate. At the end of the PLR year (cf. 5.1), the expenses incurred during the year by the PLR administration, including reimbursements to local library authorities, have first to be ascertained and deducted from the PLR fund. (The expenses, it was expected in 1982, would amount probably to between 15 and 20 per cent of the total fund.) Only after the deduction of the expenses can it be ascertained what rate per loan the remaining fund can afford to pay, which is done by dividing the sum left in the fund by the total number of grossed up loans of registered works.

The rate per loan named in the 1982 Scheme might, after these facts have been ascertained, be adjusted upwards or downwards, should the Secretary of State (for Education, the overlord of the ministry for the arts) choose to seek parliamentary approval for such a change, which would be subject to 'negative resolution' (a 'prayer' to annul or disregard it lodged within 40 days) of either House.

In 1983 the expectation was that an adjustment would be sought to the rate per loan in the autumn of 1983 (which would therefore be operative before the first payments in February 1984), probably at the same time that an amendment would be sought lowering the lower limit.

5.12 Advisory committee

In April 1982 the Registrar established an advisory committee, designed to meet roughly every two months in London. The members, who are unpaid and who have no executive function or power, include a Chief Librarian, members of the Office of Arts and Libraries (cf. 1.13) and representatives of the Association of Metropolitan Authorities, the Publishers Association, J. Whitaker & Sons, Limited (cf. 5.8), the Association of Authors' Agents, the ALCS (cf. 1.11), the Society of Authors and the Writers' Guild of Great Britain.

6 Outline of the PLR campaign

6.1 Prehistory, 1951

So far as I can now tell, John Brophy advanced his PLR proposal in 1951 (cf. 2.1) without knowing that PLR already existed in Denmark (cf. 1.2).

His proposal came closer than the Danish stock-census system to what was eventually introduced in Britain inasmuch as he proposed a payment to the author per loan, but it differed from all PLR systems in operation in that he did not suggest public funds as the source of the payments.

He proposed that the borrower should pay a fee at the time of borrowing the volume. Nine-tenths of the revenue thus raised was to go to the authors of the volumes, one-tenth to meet the cost of collecting and distributing the money.

The fee to the borrower was to be one penny (1d. in the £. s. d. currency then in use). That won the proposal the indeed catchpenny but catchy name of 'the Brophy penny'.

The social considerations that prompted the proposal were the visibly increasing poverty of authors and what was at the time believed to be the increasing affluence of borrowers. As a matter of fact, poverty in general had not been banished from Britain in 1951. Still less had it been banished for the future. It was, however, popularly and optimistically thought that it had been, and authors knew themselves to be an exception to what was considered the general rule.

It was natural, though to the next generation it might seem mistaken, that my father should look directly to the public, rather than to public funds, to pay the authors. No tradition as yet existed in Britain of state patronage of prose. The Arts Council of Great Britain was established in 1945 to distribute public funds to many arts, but literature was not among them. The Council began a (tiny) subsidy to poetry in 1950, but its patronage of prose did not begin until 1965.

In any case, my father was not seeking subsidy for literary 'merit' but payment for use by the public. His proposal simply adapted, to the benefit of the authors instead of the proprietors and at half the fee, the concept of the old commercial 'tuppenny' libraries, which were clearly by then being ousted by the public libraries (cf. 2.3).

During 1951 my father wrote frequently and spoke in many parts of Britain about his proposal, which was widely reported, applauded by many authors and several librarians and strongly opposed on two grounds.

Some librarians, though content that public libraries should collect cash fines on overdue volumes, resented their proposed rôle as penny-collectors for authors. With greater reason they feared that the titles borrowed (which had to be known if the right number of pennies was to reach the appropriate author) would have to be written down, whether by the borrower or by the library assistant, by hand.

The other objection, made by both librarians and politicians, was political. The proposal infringed the 'free'-ness of the 'free' public libraries. That is, it infringed the principle that public libraries should be a charge on the ratepayers and tax-payers but free to the borrowers at the point of borrowing.

By 1972, when WAG (Writers Action Group) was formed and began the campaign for PLR financed from central public funds, the librarians' legitimate objection to the manual recording of titles had been overtaken by automation. Knowing the prehistory, WAG emphasised the clean, electronic virtues of a loans record that could be kept at the stroke of a 'Telepen' or a 'lightpen' or an equally hygienic and convenient alternative.

However, the objection to infringement of 'the free library principle' had, by WAG's time, solidified. By 1972 it would have been politically doomed for a campaign to propose or a political party to endorse a charge to the borrower. Most members of WAG, myself included, would not have supported such a proposal even had it been feasible.

All the same, political feeling was patchy rather than on party lines. The Conservative Party, where a student of ideologies might expect to find sympathy for a charge to the borrower (and not only, he might think, to pay the authors but to support the whole public-library apparatus) was shaken by the controversy that met the introduction, by a Conservative government, of museum charges. A charge on book-borrowers was considered analogous to the charge for entrance to a museum; and museum entrance charges were, after a rocky and very brief existence under the Conservatives, abolished by the incoming Labour government in 1974.

When that Labour government eventually proposed a centrally funded PLR, the Conservative front bench, as a result of its experience with museum charges, was scarcely less solid in support of 'the free library principle' than Labour itself.

Yet in all the major parties MPs sporadically existed who wanted the borrower to be charged.

During its campaign for (emphatically) centrally funded PLR, WAG discovered how well my father had publicised his proposal. The 'Brophy penny' had entered and, indeed, stuck in folk memory. The association of my (professional and maiden) surname with WAG meant that WAG had to live down its echoes. For the most part that was a matter of countering opposition from people who wrongly supposed that WAG wanted to charge the borrower, but one person in, perhaps, a hundred was disappointed to learn that WAG was strongly against any such thing. More than one member of the public touched my heart and perplexed my conscience by sending me, as a donation to WAG, the pence they thought they ought to have been charged at the library.

Having launched and publicised his proposal, my father sought Society of Authors endorsement for it. The Society, at first reluctant, presently agreed to take up the idea but insisted that the revenue must be shared with publishers. This contradicted my father's aims in making the proposal. The Society's backing was not, however, to be had on other terms, my father could not achieve his purpose single-handed and there was in 1951 no other appropriate national body with the resources to conduct a campaign that he could approach, the Writers' Guild being still eight years short of being founded. Accordingly, my father handed over his idea but himself withdrew from the promotion of it.

6.2 Intermediate phase, 1952–72

After the handover, 'the Brophy penny' was translated into 'Public Lending Right'.

Although the latter name reflected the notion of having 'lending to the public' added to the list of the 'acts restricted by the copyright' in a copyright work (cf. 2.1), no policy was fixed on about the legislative means through which the introduction of PLR should be sought. An amendment to the 1956 Copyright Act was the favourite idea in the early 1960s and became so again in the early 1970s, but other ideas were also mooted, including an amendment to the Public Libraries and

Museums Act of 1964.

A PLR amendment to the Copyright Act of 1956 would not, of course, have benefited authors as such (cf. 1.9) but only those authors whom the Act made the first owners of the copyright in their work and who had been able to resist pressure from their publishers to assign it. Quite apart from any share of PLR that publishers might manage to take from the authors who were the copyright-owners, PLR introduced by copyright amendment would have been a direct bonus to publishers who had wrested the copyright from the author, and it would have been an inducement to more publishers to try in more cases to do so.

Neither was there any agreement on how the PLR payment, to the author or the copyright-owner as the case might be, should be calculated or on how the money should be raised. Charging the borrower fell into increasing disfavour as it became less politically feasible. Ideas were floated for a levy on the libraries themselves, despite the peril into which that would put their purchases of books.

All the same, the question of PLR, albeit in the form of an open question, was kept in the public mind, though also in the minds of librarians, who became progressively antagonised.

Between 1960 and 1964, Society of Authors propaganda for PLR was conducted largely by and under the inspiration of A. P. (Sir Alan) Herbert, author of *Public Lending Right. . . A Preliminary Memorandum Humbly Submitted to the Society of Authors*, 1960 and *Libraries: Free for All?*, 1962. He was president of the Society from 1967 to his death in 1971.

The impoverishment of authors or at least of those who belonged to the Society and answered questionnaires was established by Richard Findlater's pamphlet *The Book Writers: Who Are They?*, published by the Society in 1966, in which he reported the depressed results of a postal survey, conducted by Research Services Limited, of members' sources of income. Richard Findlater took the logically next step when he edited, in 1971, a symposium volume called *Public Lending Right: A Matter of Justice*.

The Society was represented on two major enquiries into the possibilities of PLR which reached incompatible conclusions.

The Arts Council enquiry began in 1965 and reported in 1967. It suggested that PLR payments should be financed by central government funds and based on a stock-census applying only to public libraries.

This did not inhibit Lord Eccles, the Paymaster General, who held the responsibility for the arts under a Conservative government, from setting up, in 1971, another enquiry, conducted this time by a 'working party'. Its report, known as the Working Party Report (or occasionally, after its chairman, Harry T. Hookway of the Department of Education and Science, as the Hookway Report), which was published in 1972, was not, strictly, required to recommend policy but only to state the options open to policy makers. However, it did not disguise its own inclination, which was not towards PLR but towards pseudo-PLR in the shape of the purchase-scheme (cf. 2.7). This, it suggested, should be operated under an amendment to the Copyright Act of 1956; the copyright owners should levy a charge directly on the libraries; and the Society of Authors and the Publishers Association jointly suggested, in a joint memorandum that was published as an appendix to the report, that they should together form a body to be called the Authors' and Publishers' Copyright Association that would collect and share the revenue.

6.3 WAG, 1972–82

1 The Working Party Report was officially welcomed by the Society of Authors.

A handful of Society members protested to the committee of management of the Society. PLR had been conceived as payment to authors in proportion to public use of their books. What was now proposed was payment to authors and publishers unrelated to use (but proportionate to price). The purchase-scheme was inherently less just than loans-based PLR, and it was the more unjust the older a writer was, since all the volumes that were in the libraries when it came into operation would be written off, to be lent for evermore or at least until they dropped to pieces without payment to the authors. For authors lucky enough to receive payment under the purchase-scheme, the once-only payment, made in advance of public use of the volume, was less socially beneficial than annual loans-based payments of PLR, which authors would continue to receive so long as their works continued to be borrowed. If a charge was made directly on the libraries, the copyright-owners were likely to lose as much as they gained, since the libraries would probably reduce their book purchases (the only acts on which the purchase-scheme made payment) by the amount they were obliged to spend on pseudo-PLR.

These objections to the purchase-scheme were put to the Society of Authors by five of its members by letter, which was followed by a meeting between four of us and the chairman, who, after telling us that the Society stood by the purchase-scheme and that PLR proper was not possible, either politically or in practical ways, dismissed us.

We determined to explore the feasibility of loans-sampling PLR and to solicit support for it from our fellow writers. The Society remained inflexible. In September 1972 the five of us who had made the original objection found ourselves creating a new organisation, which was named, by an early supporter who at once vanished into anonymity, Writers Action Group, whose acronym was to be spoken as 'wag'. WAG was initially intended only to urge the community of writers, inside and beyond the Society of Authors, back onto the course that would lead to PLR. At its foundation, no one foresaw a ten-year existence for it and still less that it would have to conduct the campaign for PLR.

The five founders of WAG, all professional writers, were (to list them with, in some cases, additions made after 1972):

Lettice Cooper, OBE, novelist, short-story writer, children's writer, writer of non-fiction volumes;
Francis King, OBE, FRSL, novelist, short-story writer, poet, writer of non-fiction volumes, critic;
Maureen Duffy, poet, novelist, playwright, writer of non-fiction volumes;
Sir Michael Levey, MVO, FRSL, art-historian, novelist, short-story writer, poet, writer of non-fiction volumes;
Brigid Brophy, FRSL, novelist, playwright, writer of non-fiction volumes, short-story writer, critic.

We proposed ourselves as founders simply through a common professional interest and the facts that we all conveniently lived in London and knew one another, slightly or well. (The last two listed are married to one another.)

WAG instantly laid down a firm policy: annual payments, to authors alone, from central government funds, in proportion to loans, with an additional payment on the Swedish model to cover public use of volumes held on library premises for reference (cf. 1.8).

People were invited to join WAG to promote that policy, and those who disagreed with the policy did not join. To that extent, WAG, which was always intended to be a temporary organisation, escaped policy making, though discussion of tactics was vociferous. The policy remained unchanged from 1972 to 1982 and, with the exception of the additional payment on volumes held for reference, which we failed to get, was carried out in the PLR legislation of 1979 and 1982.

WAG's first meeting was held on 29 January 1973 in a room paid for by Lettice Cooper and Jane Aiken Hodge in the handsome building the National Book League then occupied in Albemarle Street. Later meetings in London (we held some also in the North) took place, at irregular intervals, in an upper room at the Queen's Elm, Chelsea, thanks to writer-publican-WAG-member Sean Treacy.

Our chief communication line, by which we reached members who could not reach London, was the WAG newsletter, which began to be sent out, in Maureen Duffy's and my name, in 1972 and which was likewise irregular, though roughly monthly, because mailings depended on funds.

For practical purposes, WAG was run by Maureen Duffy and me, a temporary (as we thought) expedient endorsed by the first meeting. Maureen Duffy did much of the technical work, all the driving and making telephone calls and most of the attending social occasions. I wrote WAG's letters and, subject to my colleague's veto, newsletters and memoranda and, from spring 1974 onwards, typed them. The sacrifice of our time was made possible by the generosity of Michael Levey.

Although we did not always disillusion officials who supposed they were telephoning a switchboard connected to a staff of 50, WAG never had any premises except Michael Levey's and my private flat or any work force except its members, who were paying rather than paid. Only in the later years, and then only when it was swollen in anticipation of a mailing to WAG members or to Members of Parliament (to whom it was not permitted, we discovered on trying, to make bulk deliveries by hand and thus save postage) did WAG's bank balance touch the £1,000 mark (which sometimes allowed us to have the envelopes professionally addressed). By the time it achieved PLR, WAG had (or had had, since they did not all live to see the achievement) about 1,000 writer members and non-writer associate members.

2 In the winter of 1972, Maureen Duffy and I wrote in collaboration a pamphlet called *Ex Libris: The Working Writers' Report on PLR*. The sub-title marked it as WAG's reply to the Working Party Report.

We had 1,500 copies printed, under WAG's imprint, in deep, non-party-political purple covers and distributed them to MPs. The printing cost of £198 we defrayed by asking those who joined WAG during its first year for a subscription of £1, half of which was to buy a copy of *Ex Libris* and make a contribution to the publishing cost. Before 1972 was out we were able to order a run-on of 500. Occasionally we had requests for copies from libraries and other institutions. By March 1973 we had sold 37 such copies at 20p apiece, including one to the New Zealand Parliament. I reported this information in the WAG newsletter along with the encouraging news that New Zealand was about to institute centrally funded PLR.

Maureen Duffy made contact with four manufacturers of automated data-capture equipment, through whom we became familiar with electronic methods of recording an ISBN printed (or inserted) in the volume either in bar code (a strip of parallel black and white bars of different thicknesses which the instrument is passed across and translates into the digits the strip encodes) or in characters both readable by eye and recordable by machine. She also made contact with three computer consultants, one of them Logica (cf. 1.7 and 5.6), all of whom gave us outlines, drawn up to our specifications, of computerised loans-sampling systems. Thus by 1973 we were able to prove that WAG's policy could be put into operation.

The late Edward Hyams urged us to produce a one-page leaflet addressed to the public. In 1973 we had 12,000 copies printed and persuaded many central libraries to put them on their counters. Other WAG members insinuated them not only into libraries but into medical waiting rooms and banks.

We began to make contact with MPs. I wrote to Will (who was known to some of his other friends as Bill) Hamling, Labour MP for Woolwich West, whom I had seen but not spoken to on a public occasion. He invited Maureen Duffy and me to tea at the House, where he declared himself a friend of my father's, and from 1972 until his death in March 1975 he regularly invited us to sit with him over a tray in the canteen, where he introduced us to every MP, of every party, who entered and we then propagandised for PLR on the WAG model.

As PLR was not an occasion of party-political conflict (cf. 6.1), WAG was not tempted to develop party-political leanings. Many WAG members, including the founders, had pronounced political convictions, but the only consensus between them was to the effect that to party-politicise WAG would be to undermine the all-party support we had begun to collect for WAG policy.

We were, however, often dependent on the influence of an individual WAG member either with an individual MP or (for example, that of John Hibbs with the Liberal Party) with a political group in or beyond Parliament.

We owed to the generosity of Penelope Wallace our supply of relevant parliamentary papers. Alastair Service explained, so far as it was explicable, parliamentary procedure. Margaret Yorke supplied information about libraries. Dulan Barber, besides undertaking many on his own account, let Maureen Duffy and me pass on to him several of our publicity and organisational chores.

Joan Tate kept us informed of developments in the socio-economics of authorship in Sweden. James Brockway did the same in relation to Holland. In 1976 Maureen Duffy and I visited Holland, as guests of the Dutch writers' union, to discuss and lecture on PLR.

Brigadier Peter Young, DSO, MC and bar was eager to put his martial expertise at WAG's disposal and several times offered to lead WAG in a commando raid.

In 1973 Maureen Duffy and I approached the Joseph Rowntree Social Service Trust, which in 1974 made WAG a grant of £750, which was followed in 1976 by an unsolicited £100. These deeply welcome gifts were the only substantial sums WAG ever received from a source other than its members, who were generous in both cash and labour. Several times a batch of envelopes for a mailing was addressed, and once stamped, by WAG members, many of whom paid above the asking price (£1 for writers, 50p for non-writer associates) for their yearly subscriptions.

Members also expended ingenuity on fund-raising for WAG. Ted Hughes suggested and offered to participate in a reading of work by WAG authors. It took place on 24 January 1974 at the Queen's Elm and was followed by a series of occasional readings of verse and prose by WAG contributors to mainly WAG audiences, who paid silver into WAG funds at the door. Frederic Raphael conceived, introduced and edited a volume of essays, *Bookmarks*, which Cape published in 1974 and Quartet in 1975, to which all the contributors were WAG authors and all, including the editor, abdicated their royalties in favour of WAG. Madelaine Duke, a registered silversmith as well as a novelist, made and gave to WAG a silver pendant for which, at her suggestion, we offered raffle tickets through the newsletter, which disclosed that most of our members were addicted gamblers. Two members, Martin Booth and John Mercer, produced the spontaneous suggestion in 1973 of a fund-raising sale of WAG members' manuscripts and signed copies. We asked in the newsletter for promises and were overwhelmed by actual parcels, which we eventually sold to a bookseller to the benefit of WAG finances.

3 The Society of Authors accepted a proposal by B. S. Johnson, a member of WAG, that a 'working party' (a term evidently then in vogue) should 'reconsider' the Society's constitution, which dated from 1908. The proposal was for a working party of ten, elected from and by Society members. To those the Society's committee of management added five of its own nominees. The elected members included six members of WAG, and we sat, under B. S. Johnson's chairmanship, once a fortnight from March to July 1973. The (un-'reconsidered') constitution of the Society did not oblige the Society to heed the recommendations that emerged and, in the event, it did not. Yet Bryan Johnson, who committed suicide in November 1973, was, perhaps, posthumously, one of the causes of the changes of character and status which the Society presently undertook, in the light of which the story of its quarrel with WAG can be told without bitterness.

In November 1972 the Society attacked WAG in the *Bookseller*. Maureen Duffy and I replied. The attack was repeated, together with an anti-WAG editorial but without WAG's reply, in the Society's journal, which went out with the ballot papers for the elections to the committee of management in March 1973, in which four members of WAG were candidates. The WAG candidates could not rebut the attack directly to the electorate since the Society did not make the addresses of its members available to their fellow members, so Francis King inserted a 'personal' advertisement in *The Times* urging the voters to read WAG's reply in the *Bookseller* before voting. Given the circumstances we accounted it an unexpected triumph that one of the WAG candidates, Giles Gordon, was elected and that the WAG candidates as a whole took between 30 and 40 per cent of the vote; their precise percentage was hard to calculate because the certified voting figures sent out to candidates contained, Maureen Duffy noticed, a discrepancy of some 600 non-existent votes and the final figures had to be adjusted.

In mid-1973 we tried to penetrate the veil by taking advertising space in three literary periodicals and publishing, with their consent, the names (in three sections) of the members of WAG, who still numbered only a few hundred but who now included some of the most distinguished and some of the most famous writers in Britain. One of the advertisements was paid for, a week before he died, by John Creasey.

At the Society of Authors AGM in July 1973, two WAG members, A. L. Barker and Nicholas Wollaston, won a majority for a proposal that the Society should postally ballot its members on their preference between the purchase-scheme and WAG's policy of loans-sampling PLR. The unreformed constitution did not, however, bind the Society to act on the motion.

The Society meanwhile pursued the purchase-scheme by having a private Member's Bill drafted. When Maureen Duffy and I went to see the solicitor who was drafting it, we were accompanied by Bruce Douglas-Mann, a solicitor and, in 1973, a Labour MP, who acted in this case as WAG's solicitor and then generously waived his fee.

The Society's draft Bill proposed to amend the Copyright Act of 1956 and thereby benefit copyright-owners rather than authors as such; it would implement the purchase-scheme and, although as a private Bill it could not deal explicitly with money, it planned to make a charge either on the rates or directly on the libraries; the charge would be levied and collected by a company to be set up jointly by the publishers and the Society of Authors.

It was to outflank this threat that, at Maureen Duffy's suggestion, WAG formed a collecting society for authors alone. Several WAG members contributed cash and bought shares, but ultimately the society had to be reconstituted as a company limited by guarantee and not having a share capital, in which form it became the ALCS (cf. 1.11). The reconstitution was under the generous guidance of Anton Felton, accountant, and Jack Black, solicitor. It was partly paid for by money derived ultimately from my father, which I considered appropriate because one of the aims of the collecting society from the outset was to secure for its members their German PLR. To that end Maureen Duffy and I visited VG WORT in Munich in 1976, but it took another four years and diplomatic effort by Ted Willis to achieve the object.

In October 1973 the Publishers Association held a reception at the St Ermin's Hotel to launch the purchase-scheme private Bill that had been drafted. The MPs who attended included several WAG friends, among them Will Hamling (cf. 6.3, 2). Of the roughly 50 authors present, about half were members of WAG who had wrung invitations from their publishers or, like Maureen Duffy and myself, from Lord Goodman. Asked by the organisers to make the launching speech at the reception, Lord Goodman astonished them and delighted WAG by insisting that all present send a unanimous telegram to Lord Eccles demanding central funds to finance PLR.

4 From the end of 1972 WAG engaged the interest of the press. We began as a target of frequent attack, which usually repeated the Society of Authors' accusation that we were a tiny minority 'rocking the boat'. Even this often gave Maureen Duffy and me the opportunity to reply with an explanation of the crucial difference between the purchase-scheme and loans-sampling PLR. Quickly we became known as sources of information about the techniques and, from 1976 onwards, the parliamentary progress of PLR.

Quite apart from giving information to enquirers on the telephone, between 1972 and 1982 Maureen Duffy and I took part more times than can now (or, indeed, could then) be counted in radio (including overseas radio) and television programmes, including news bulletins; we spoke at conferences and gave lectures and talks all over Britain; we wrote innumerable articles and papers. For a few of these activities we were paid, and our earnings went into WAG funds, though only once was I paid, by a national daily, a large enough fee to finance an entire mailing of the WAG newsletter.

The developing complexities of PLR were, over the decade of struggle, accurately and continuously reported by the *Bookseller,* by Douglas Hill in *Tribune,* by Peter Lewis in the *Daily Mail* and by Robert Leeson in *Morning Star.* The most mangled accounts were given in a magazine that devoted an issue to the subject in December 1975 and, frequently, in the

116

House of Commons. Future historians of PLR would be wise not to accept without corroboration the accuracy of any contemporary newspaper report.

5 From early 1973 WAG was winning the support of other organisations. English PEN allowed us to use its addressing machine and circularise its members. The Crime Writers' Association took up our PLR policy and reported progress to its members. On a proposal by Dudley Barker, the London Freelance Branch of the NUJ endorsed loans sampling. Women in Media asked Maureen Duffy and me to talk to them and joined WAG *en bloc*. George Mikes, as chairman of PEN in Exile, arranged in June 1973 for us to speak to a PEN meeting. William Garner and Maureen Duffy made contact with writers' organisations in West Germany (which at that time had PLR legislation but not yet functioning PLR) and, when Dieter Lattman visited London in November 1973, the German Institute mounted an exposition, from which WAG emerged the better, of the purchase-scheme by the Society of Authors and of loans-sampling PLR by WAG. Early in 1974 loans sampling was endorsed by the Writers' Guild of Great Britain.

Reg Davis-Poynter, publisher and associate member of WAG, assembled 14 publisher signatures to a letter renouncing and discountenancing a publishers' share in PLR. It was not published, but we sent copies widely, including one to the minister for the arts.

Maureen Duffy and I addressed the arts committee of the Parliamentary Labour Party and in the autumn of 1973 it adopted loans sampling as its PLR policy. This was the first major political commitment WAG won.

6 Within WAG, a movement began in 1973 towards the unionisation of book writers in Britain. Not all WAG members were part of this movement, and WAG continued its campaign for PLR independently of it. Gordon Williams proposed at a WAG meeting that those members who were interested in unionisation should explore the possibilities. A group under the chairmanship of John Braine and the secretaryship of Joyce Marlow held meetings at the house of the late Paul Tabori, and smaller groups of us sought interviews with unions of journalists, printers, managerial staff and scriptwriters to discover which unions were prepared to take in book writers (virtually all, it turned out) and on what terms.

It was through the contact we made in this way with

ASTMS (Association of Scientific, Technical and Managerial Staffs) that we met Ron Pluck, who became WAG's and eventually the British PLR system's statistician (cf. 1.7).

Written reports on all the appropriate unions that were prepared to admit writers of books were sent to all WAG members, together with papers for a postal ballot. The vote opted for the Writers' Guild of Great Britain, a union affiliated to the TUC (Trades Union Congress) but not to any political party. Founded in 1959 as the Screenwriters' Guild, it had, under the name Writers' Guild, become a union of writers for radio, television and films. It attracted the WAG voters as a small union, whose members not only formed policy but carried it out themselves, doing, for example, their own negotiating, and because its membership was largely 'self-employed' and therefore conversant with the problems that went with that status (cf. 2.5).

In response to WAG's knock at its door, the Guild amended its membership rules in 1974 to admit also writers of books, poetry, short stories and plays for the stage. It co-opted several WAG writers, including Maureen Duffy and me, onto its executive council for a year, after which book writers and dramatists stood for annual election to a number of seats that the new rules reserved to them.

Although many active members of WAG were, from 1974 onwards, active members and office holders in the Writers' Guild, there were WAG members with no wish to join the Guild, and WAG's non-writer associate members were not eligible to join even had they wanted to. WAG therefore maintained its entirely separate and independent existence and pursued the campaign for PLR, though the separate existence of the WG (Writers' Guild) and WAG, often with representatives or spokesmen in common, caused confusion in the outside (and occasionally in the inside) world.

Thus WAG, itself transient, set in train in 1973 movements that led to two permanent results (apart from British PLR itself): the creation of the ALCS as a collecting society for all writers, whose members began receiving their German PLR before anyone had seen any British PLR; and the opportunity for any book writers in Britain who wanted to do so to join a trade union.

In 1978, four years after the Writers' Guild opened its membership to book writers and dramatists, the Society of Authors did what Bryan Johnson had presumably been urging it to do and made itself into a trade union, too, though not one affiliated to the TUC.

Soon after the accession of the book writers, the Writers' Guild negotiated a card-sharing agreement with the NUJ (National Union of Journalists) and began the task (in which the Society of Authors joined forces with the Guild in 1980) of negotiating minimum-terms agreements with publishers of books. These, by stipulating a floor beneath which the publisher undertook not to descend in the terms accorded the writer in the publishing contract, gave book writing members of the Guild the same type of protection that the Guild had already secured for its television-writer members through minimum-terms agreements with the television companies.

7 In the autumn of 1973, Michael Holroyd, as the new chairman of the Society of Authors, inaugurated a policy of politeness to WAG. This he pursued by inviting us to agree on a fair wording for the mooted postal ballot of Society members (cf. 6.3, 3), demanding that WAG pay part of the cost of the ballot, which WAG neither could nor would do, and asking Maureen Duffy and me to provide a version of our loans-sampling project in entirely non-technical language, which we did.

The Publishers Association asked us to support a 'neutral' version of the draft private Member's Bill, leaving the decision to be taken later and in private between the purchase-scheme and PLR proper. We refused, because WAG could support nothing except PLR.

The draft Bill was adopted by Ernle Money, a Conservative MP who had won fourth place in the ballot for private Members' Bills, a position that gave him some, though if he did not secure government backing not very great, hope of getting the measure onto the statute book.

Maureen Duffy then booked the Caxton Hall for 31 January 1974. We began with a lobby of the House of Commons. One hundred and forty WAG authors assembled in dusk and mud opposite, and crossed to the House, where we talked to MPs in a committee room booked for the purpose by WAG-author Michael Foot, MP. In the evening we held a public meeting in Caxton Hall, under the chairmanship of Lord Willis.

Against a backdrop, painted by Michael Levey's and my daughter, of the names of WAG's now 498 members, our guest speakers were Lord Goodman and Philip Hughes, chairman of Logica, who affirmed the feasibility of computerised PLR. Our WAG speakers were Reg Davis-Poynter, who affirmed that publishers should take no share of PLR (cf. 6.3, 5), and John Braine, who spoke, as a librarian turned author, in the cause of author-librarian reconciliation.

In the same cause we demonstrated from the platform the clean and convenient use of a 'Telepen' lent us for the purpose by S & B Electronics (cf. 6.1) in automatically recording an ISBN.

We were also authorised, on condition that we attributed it to anonymous 'representatives of the library profession', to read out a message that 'provided the money for PLR comes from central government funds and goes to authors (rather than publishers), librarians would be prepared to provide reasonable co-operation in researching and operating a loans-sampling scheme, and a lot of the opposition to PLR that has existed in the past will die away'.

We read out to the meeting telegrams in support of WAG and loans-based PLR from J. B. Priestley, George Melly, John Fowles, Malcolm Saville, Frank Kermode, Ronald Duncan, Denise Robins, Harold Pinter and Roy Fuller and a cable from Antibes: 'To accept totally inequitable purchase right would be to sell future finally for mess of burnt pottage – Graham Greene'.

When the audience of 300 left, the late J. G. Farrell (one of WAG's two Booker prize-winning members) found himself in possession of a pair of black gloves (f.) for whose owner we advertised in the newsletter.

The hoped-for (as it remained, rather than actual) peace with the librarians was not the only reconciliation we could announce to the meeting. On the day before, the Society of Authors told us that it had had our computerised plan for loans sampling examined by a computer firm, as a result of which the Society now endorsed loans sampling. This the Society announced publicly in a letter to *The Times* and to its members in its journal in the spring. It asked the WAG proposers of a postal ballot of its members' preference to withdraw their motion, which, as they replied, they could not do, since it had been passed by an AGM. The ballot was in fact never held.

Although some columnists (for instance, in *The Times* of 7 February) pursued the vendetta, maintaining, for instance, that the Society was pressing 'the case for justice' while having to 'fight off the attacks by Miss Brigid Brophy and her group', WAG's campaign for centrally funded loans-based PLR in fact had the loyal support of the Society of Authors from 1 February 1974 onwards. The reconciliation continued under the chairmanship (1974–5) of Lady Antonia Fraser, who presently joined WAG, and was cemented when one of WAG's founders, Francis King, held the chairmanship of the Society from 1975 to 1977.

We had now only to win over the British government.

8 WAG's first minister for the arts was Viscount Eccles, with whom Edward Hyams, Maureen Duffy and I, accompanied by one of WAG's computer advisers, had a meeting in October 1973 and whom we found sceptical both of computerised PLR and of the benefit of PLR to authors. Lord Eccles presently retired from his ministry, where he was replaced by Norman St John-Stevas, with whom I had a slight acquaintance made while taking part in television and with no PLR connexions.

The first meeting to which the new minister summoned Maureen Duffy and me, and to which we took a statistical report on loans sampling written at heroically short notice by R. A. Pluck, was a large one, attended also by Lord Goodman, Denis de Freitas, OBE (then legal adviser to the Performing Right Society, later chairman of the British Copyright Council) and the Society of Authors. Norman St John-Stevas told us that he intended to supplant the Ernle Money private Bill by government legislation, which would introduce the purchase-scheme and probably place at least some of the charge on the rates. We said we could not advise writers or MPs to support a Bill of that kind.

A couple of days after the meeting a newspaper reported an ostensible 'leak' to the effect that WAG had capitulated to the purchase-scheme. Maureen Duffy and I saw the report while we were preaching loans sampling to a meeting at Ruislip, from which we telephoned a denial. The newspaper presently made us full amends by publishing a complete and correct account of the difference between the purchase-scheme and PLR.

From Norman St John-Stevas's threat to impose the purchase-scheme authors were almost immediately delivered by the dissolution of Parliament in preparation for a general election, which also swallowed up the Ernle Money private Bill.

The Conservative government was replaced by Labour. The Ernle Money private Bill was replaced by one sponsored by the Conservative MP Kenneth Baker, who told us, when we sought a meeting with him, that he did not intend to commit himself or his Bill to a decision between PLR and the purchase-scheme.

The new minister for the arts was Hugh Jenkins (later Lord Jenkins of Putney), for whom Maureen Duffy and I had campaigned in his Putney constituency during the general election, whom, as non-party organisers of WAG, we had met during his shadow period and to whom we had, we thought, explained the difference between the purchase-scheme and loans-sampling PLR.

He began his ministry by summoning a large meeting, which Reg Davis-Poynter, Maureen Duffy and I attended on behalf of WAG. Before everyone at the table he placed written 'proposals for legislation'. They consisted of the purchase-scheme. As we reported in the WAG newsletter, Lord Goodman's response was 'volcanic'.

However, the previous minister had arranged a meeting between WAG's statistical and computer advisers and those of the Department of Education and Science (DES), and that was allowed to go ahead in March 1974. WAG pressed for the Library Association (LA) to be invited. The DES refused, and we feared it would thereby unravel the reconciliation with the LA that we had been weaving. The only clear advantage to authors in the arrival of a Labour minister for the arts was that he agreed with WAG's insistence on central funding.

In May 1974 Hugh Jenkins enlarged the technical meetings into a Technical Investigation Group (TIG). This time the LA was represented, along with the Publishers Association and the local authorities. In August even writers were added. Both WAG and the Society of Authors were thereafter represented on TIG, and Maureen Duffy toiled in the cause of PLR against the preference for the purchase-scheme of the numerous civil servants.

TIG's first brief was to examine and cost WAG's plan for loans sampling, including the addition designed to pay the authors of reference stock (cf. 1.8). To this was added a brief to examine and cost also the purchase-scheme.

The report, besides establishing (again) that loans sampling was feasible, established that, even with the high cost of the comparatively huge sample then supposed necessary, loans sampling would not cost any more to set up and operate than the purchase-scheme.

The report to this effect was ready by October 1974, though its publication was postponed. Hugh Jenkins required field tests and further research to be undertaken and he commissioned Logica to design and carry out a programme. This prolonged TIG's life (and Maureen Duffy's unpaid hard labour) by a year and led to a 'final' TIG report, which was in effect an addendum, a year after the main report.

Since, however, WAG's PLR system had been vindicated by October 1974, and since it now had the unanimous support of the writers' organisations, we expected legislation (and loans-sampling legislation at that), especially since the Queen's Speech of 29 October 1974 listed in the government's legislative programme 'a Bill. . . to provide PLR for authors'.

Harried in the House of Commons by two of WAG's MP allies, Andrew Faulds and Bruce Douglas-Mann, the government said it hoped to make an announcement of some kind before Christmas 1974.

The (private) announcement that reached us before Christmas from Hugh Jenkins was, however, surprising: he was still, despite TIG, undecided between the purchase-scheme and PLR proper but, whichever he decided to introduce, he intended to make the payment to the author proportionate to the selling-price of the volume, on the grounds that 'a life's work of 800 pages justifies a higher payment than an essay of 50 pages'. Maureen Duffy and I hurriedly assembled armfuls of volumes (some of them, ironically, by WAG-founder Michael Levey) that demonstrated the fact that short texts may be highly priced and long ones low-priced and took them to a meeting with Hugh Jenkins on 3 December. He later publicly and honourably admitted that we had dissuaded him from this bizarre item. He asked us, however, what our reaction would be to the offer of 'the purchase-scheme or nothing'. We rejected the dilemma as artificial and declared ourselves equally determined not to have the purchase-scheme and to have loans-sampling PLR. Some months later Hugh Jenkins told us, though only in private, that he had now become convinced of the superiority of loans-sampling PLR.

9 By April 1975 there was still no word of a government Bill. WAG therefore mounted the first open-air demonstration by writers in Britain. For the date we picked 23 April because it was St George's Day and Shakespeare's putative birthday (arrived at by turning the calendar back from his recorded

baptism on 26 April 1564).

Though it later moved into the DES building at Waterloo, in 1975 the Office of Arts and Libraries had its premises in Belgrave Square. With police permission, the WAG writers, supported by members of the Writers' Guild and the Society of Authors, assembled on the large traffic island opposite. Ted Willis addressed them through a loud-hailer we had hired. So did Jacquetta Hawkes, a WAG author who had travelled from, appropriately, Stratford-on-Avon.

In mid-morning, two actors, whom Joyce Marlow had put us in touch with, dressed as St George and the dragon (to the latter of whom Maureen Duffy had added a hand-made tail) in costumes borrowed from the Tower Theatre by courtesy of WAG associate member Sara Randall, mounted the portico of the ministry and handed in a bouquet of the red roses of England with a note imploring Hugh Jenkins to save English literature from extinction.

Throughout the afternoon WAG and Guild writers tramped round Belgrave Square. The WAG banner was made and carried by Gillian Freeman and Edward Thorpe. Placards of genuine Shakespearean quotation ('in delay there lies no plenty') contended with an entirely fake diatribe in blank verse against civil servants inscribed on his by Colin Spencer (who in 1982 became co-chairman of the Writers' Guild). Bill Craig (who in 1982 became president of the Writers' Guild) was credited with the highest number of circuits of the square.

In May there was still no government Bill. Ted Willis decided to nudge the government into action by introducing a PLR Bill as a private measure in the Lords. The text was drafted for us by a generous barrister, and in July 1975 it was introduced by Lord Willis. Since, without government backing, it had no hope of progressing further, Ted Willis withdrew it, but not before he had used the occasion gracefully and adroitly to win the sympathy of the Lords for PLR, a sympathy that was never forfeited, and to elicit a reiteration of the government's commitment to legislate itself.

10 Not until the spring of 1976 did the government introduce its Bill, which incorporated WAG's policy except in relation to reference stock and other-than-public libraries.

Hugh Jenkins was replaced as arts minister by Lord Donaldson of Kingsbridge.

The Bill was introduced with only just enough time in

hand to complete all its stages within the Session, in default of which it was bound to fall. A preliminary project to take it directly to its committee stage (normally the third, if one counts the purely formal first reading as the first) in the House of Commons failed, because government and opposition, though they agreed on the Bill, could not agree on the parliamentary terms of the manoeuvre, and the Bill was, unusually, taken to the House of Lords before going to the House of Commons. Under tactful guidance from Lord Willis, it completed its second reading on 5 April 1976, its committee stage on 27 April and its report and third reading on 11 May. It arrived in the Commons on 25 May for its second reading, which was adjourned.

Several WAG authors attended several debates. Jüri Gabriel attended all, and Brenda Naylor most of, the committee stages in the House of Commons. Maureen Duffy and I attended the whole of every debate and every committee sitting in the Commons both of the 1976 Bill and of the 1978–9 Bill. We owed our tickets for the public enclosure 'under the gallery' to Ted Willis in the House of Lords and, in the House of Commons, usually to Jo Richardson, Labour MP and staunch friend of PLR, and occasionally to the arts section of the Conservative research organisation, with which we were on friendly terms and through whom we briefed the Conservative front bench. I reported everything we heard and saw, in detail of a type not recorded in Hansard, in the WAG newsletter.

When the Bill reached the Commons it became quickly clear that three backbenchers (two Conservative and one Labour) planned a filibuster (cf. 1.3). In the later stages they acquired five further Conservative adjutants. Those MPs who had not been approached by WAG or by WAG constituents were plainly baffled by PLR and by the government's Bill, which several of them did not know to be a government Bill. Because the arts minister sat in the Lords, the handling of the Bill in the Commons was tossed to a variety of junior ministers, none of whom had apparently had time to master the subject or the content of the Bill. The exchanges in the chamber often gave the impression of the bewildered offering explanations to the bewildered.

Resumed on 26 May at short notice (which obliged WAG author Tim Jeal to rush his MP to the House), the second reading was again adjourned, at midnight. There were resumptions and adjournments on 24 June and 5 July.

Before the October resumption, WAG authors, wearing 'PLR now' stickers handed out by Ray Jenkins, chairman of the Writers' Guild, lobbied MPs. Kingsley Amis smiled at and Sir (as he presently became) Angus Wilson addressed MPs from a WAG platform in a committee room secured for us by Jo Richardson and the Conservative MP John Hannam. Our hope was to make sure that the 100 MPs needed to vote for the closure at the next debate would be present.

Soon after 10 p.m. on 14 October, however, the closure was lost, as only 99 MPs were present to vote for it (to one MP against). The debate therefore continued, the filibustering MPs trying, by the length and pointlessness of their speeches, to bore MPs out of the House, the government whip and friend to PLR, A. W. (Jock) Stallard, trying to keep them in it. At about 1.45 a.m. on what had become 15 October, the Bill achieved its second reading, by 99 votes to nil.

The Bill moved, on 26 October, to standing committee, on which the three main filibustering MPs, as well as several friends of PLR, sat. The filibuster used up the first (morning) sitting; three sittings (morning, afternoon and post-9 p.m.) on 28 October; the morning and afternoon sittings on 2 November but not the sitting due to begin at 9 p.m. and expected to last all night, because it proved, with their active and giggling help as they ducked in and out of the area in which an MP was accounted present, inquorate; and morning, afternoon and evening sittings on 4 November. On 9 November there was a change. The filibuster group agreed to let the Bill complete its committee stage. But the parliamentary Session had dangerously few days left to run.

The Bill returned to the floor of the Commons, for its report and third reading, on 16 November and met a giggling filibuster of eight, each of whom was prepared to talk boringly for up to 45 minutes, a stratagem that gave the rest of the filibuster the chance of a kip and that enforced silence on the friends of PLR as the only way of giving the Bill a chance to pass. The government had put on a two-line whip, the Conservatives none. By a quarter to midnight it was no longer possible to muster 100 MPs to vote for the closure. The debate or, rather, filibuster did not end until the government adjourned it at 1.45 a.m. Only two days of the Parliamentary Session remained, and the Bill was lost.

11 'I shook with anger for 15 hours.' Thus we quoted Angus

Wilson in the WAG newsletter. One of WAG's publisher members, Christopher MacLehose, acted out his anger and won the applause of WAG writers by rejecting a manuscript proffered for publication by one of the filibustering MPs.

WAG members believed that eight callous and frivolous men in well-paid jobs had destroyed the authors' hope of fair pay, wasted the money and effort they had put into the campaign and frustrated the will of Parliament and the united will, as it by then officially was, of the Labour, Conservative, Liberal, Scottish National and Plaid Cymru parties.

Although we explored, during 1977, the possibilities of PLR by 'administrative arrangement' instead of through legislation and even drew up a plan, our best hope was that the government would introduce another Bill. Five WAG writers (Kingsley Amis, Angus Wilson, Elizabeth Jane Howard, Maureen Duffy and I) wrote to the prime minister, James Callaghan, asking to see him. He bade us to 10 Downing Street. We enlarged our party to include also Francis King, Dame Veronica Wedgwood and Antonia Fraser, and were received on 17 May 1977 with the utmost sympathy but, as a result of the government's precarious majority and the threat of a renewed filibuster, small optimism.

WAG continued to campaign. Eva Figes suggested that WAG writers with forthcoming books and acquiescent publishers should preface their work with a brief notice about PLR, and many did so, though some, like Warren Tute, had to tussle with the publishers concerned.

Andrew Faulds, MP, from time to time a Labour arts spokesman and an early and firm friend to PLR, gave me the opportunity to write the papers for a Council of Europe discussion of PLR and recommendation of centrally funded loans sampling. In November 1977, Ted Willis, Maureen Duffy and I spent three days in Strasbourg, taking part in talks and an international seminar, and in the next month the PLR recommendation was presented by Andrew Faulds and adopted by the Council of Europe.

Two WAG writers, John Tully and Maureen Duffy, became co-chairman of the Writers' Guild in 1978. In September of that year, Maureen Duffy, as the Guild's representative at the Trades Union Congress at Brighton, proposed a motion calling on the government to implement PLR without delay and won for PLR the support of the trade-union movement, only one union dissenting.

Suddenly, the government introduced another (though textually substantially unchanged) PLR Bill.

It had its second reading in the House of Commons on 10 November 1978. The filibuster was in full flower, but the feeling the Bill from the first induced about its fate was quite different from the uncertainty that had surrounded the Bill of 1976. While the vote was taken on the second reading James Callaghan came and sat briefly with Maureen Duffy and me in the enclosure under the gallery. The filibuster raised such a din that even he was for a second unable to tell the outcome of the vote, but the Bill proved to have passed its second reading.

The junior ministers to whom the Bill was entrusted, John Smith, QC (who was lost to PLR after the second reading thanks to his promotion to the cabinet) and Gordon Oakes, were well-informed and effective. Most important of all, Michael Foot, as Leader of the House, took command of the parliamentary events. He amassed an arsenal of procedural methods, most of which he never needed to use except as bargaining counters, for containing, but not stifling and thus provoking, the filibuster.

The Bill proceded unerringly, as I reported for the WAG newsletter and also for the *Bookseller* stage by stage. Its committee stage took two days (21 and 23 November), its third reading and report three (6 December 1978 and 24 and 30 January 1979). The Bill went to the House of Lords and the steering touch of Ted Willis on 12 February, when it had its second reading there. Its committee stage was on 20 February and it was finally passed, as the result of the strategy designed and executed by Michael Foot, on 6 March 1979.

Michael Foot sent Maureen Duffy and me copies of what was now the Act with inscriptions describing us as its authors. On 15 March he gave a party at the Privy Council offices for the MPs and some of the writers who had contributed to the victory. Bill Craig, who had tramped round Belgrave Square with a placard, now bore upstairs a cake which Maureen Duffy and I had had baked for Michael Foot in the not entirely naturalistic likeness of the open statute book, on which icing inscribed 'PLR'.

WAG's own celebration, to whose cost the members subscribed, had to wait until a newsletter had recounted the details of the triumph and appointed the date, 1 June. The organisation was entrusted to Kay Dick, one of WAG's most ardent and active authors, and she chose to hold the WAG party at (cf. 6.3, 3) the St Ermin's Hotel.

12 WAG and its newsletter went into suspended animation. The newsletter's policy had been to report to the whole membership all the deeds (recruiting, publicity, solicitation of or argument with MPs, fund-raising), all the concerns (even when they were peripheral to WAG's main purpose, like the campaign by David Benedictus and Ben Whitaker for an extension of copyright to the common benefit of creators) and all the facts-and-figures-type information that each WAG member reported to us. At the same time, the newsletter gave an entirely frank report of all our discussions with civil servants and politicians. Even when the needs of negotiation kept it silent temporarily, it recounted the whole truth as soon as it was free to do so. The only item we suppressed was, at his request, the closeness and helpfulness to WAG of Airey Neave, MP, to whom WAG author Pauline Neville introduced us in 1975 and who continued to promote WAG's cause until his murder in 1979.

There was, however, a conflict between the full and frank detail of the newsletter and WAG funds. To save postage and duplicating costs, I typed the newsletter on stencils in single spacing. It was reproduced on both sides of foolscap sheets of rather fibrous paper. Each issue was preceded by a key to its space-saving code, which consisted not only of initials for almost everyone and everything but of a device whereby 'W Jane Austen' meant 'WAG author Jane Austen', 'WW Jane Austen' meant 'WAG and Writers' Guild author Jane Austen' and 'Wa Cassandra Austen' meant 'WAG associate member Cassandra Austen'. To some recipients these devices gave the newsletter its idiosyncratic tone. To others, with poor sight or no taste for cryptography, they made it unreadable.

WAG remained in nominal existence after the passage of the Act. With representatives of the Society of Authors and my fellow representatives of the Writers' Guild, I (as WW BB, in newsletter code) took part in the consultations with authors enjoined by the 1979 Act on the civil servants devising the Scheme (cf. 1.13). The consultations were last-minute and conducted under the threat of a disruption of the already in fact dislocated (cf. 5.2) PLR timetable, which could not afford a moment's further slip if authors were to receive the promised first payments in 1984. We did not manage to carry all our points but we carried several, without which the Scheme would be even more of a maze than it is.

I wrote the last WAG newsletter, for mailing which WAG had kept cash in hand, in April 1982. It recounted the parliamentary approval given to the Scheme in April by a House of Commons committee (witnessed by Maureen Duffy) and by the House of Lords (witnessed by me), detailed the contents of the Scheme and gave notice that WAG, as it had always meant to do when its main purpose was achieved, would now autodestruct.

However, many active members of WAG were already, and remained, active members of the Writers' Guild, the ALCS and the Society of Authors. The truce made between WAG and the Society during the PLR campaign (cf. 6.3, 7) was succeeded by an alliance between the Guild and the Society, who jointly took responsibility for the ALCS (cf. 1.11), jointly took up the Guild's quest for minimum-terms agreements with publishers (cf. 6.3, 6) and in 1983 jointly urged on the government the improvements to the PLR system listed in 4, 3.

13 There was a bizarre codetta on 17 September 1982, when the *Times Literary Supplement* published a letter attacking the principle and practice of PLR from Mr Godfrey Carter, who said that in 1975, when he was 'a member of the Office of Parliamentary Counsel', it was his 'misfortune' to draft the PLR Bill. The *TLS* published a short reply from Francis King on 24 September 1982 and a slightly longer one from me on 1 October.

Works consulted

Dietz, Adolf: *Le Droit d'Auteur dans la Communauté Européenne* (XII/125/76–F), 1976, unpublished study undertaken for the EEC. *The Public Lending Right in the Federal Republic of Germany: Evolution and Regulation*, unpublished paper delivered at Oxford, 1976. *The Social Endeavours of Writers and Artists and the Copyright Law*. Munich, 1972: Max Planck Institute for Foreign and International Patent, Copyright and Competition Law. Reprint of pp. 451–71, No. 4/1972, of International Review of Industrial Property and Copyright Law.

Gedin, Per: *Literature in the Market Place*, translated by George Bisset. London, 1977: Faber.

Gehlin, Jan: *The Swedish Writer and his Rights*, translated by Paul Britten Austin. Sweden, 1973: The Swedish Institute.

Legat, Michael: *An Author's Guide to Publishing*. London, 1982: Robert Hale.

Mann, Peter: *Bookshop Provision in Yorkshire*. Unpublished study, 1975, carried out with the aid of a grant from the Yorkshire Arts Association.

Sutherland, J. A.: *Fiction and the Fiction Industry*. London, 1978: University of London, Athlone Press.

Taylor, L. J. (compiler): *A Librarian's Handbook*. London, 1976: The Library Association.

Torfing, Grethe: *A Co-operative Library System: Danish Public Libraries*. Ballerup, 1977: Bibliotekscentralens Forlag.

Whale, R. F.: *Copyright*. London, 1971: Longman.

Wiesand, Andreas Johannes in collaboration with Karla Fohrbeck: *Literature and the Public in the Federal Republic of Germany*. Munich, 1976: Carl Hanser Verlag.

Reports and corporate and composite documents

CISAC, un demi-siècle 1926–1976. Paris, 1976: Confédération Internationale des Sociétés d'Auteurs et Compositeurs

Copyright and Designs Law. Report of the Committee to consider the law on copyright and designs chaired by the Honourable Mr Justice Whitford. Cmnd. 6732. London, 1977: HMSO.

Lending Right. Unpublished papers (by A. Françon, Mario

Fabiani, Pirkko-Liisa Aro, W. Weincke, Herman Cohen Jehoram, J. H. Spoor, Adolf Dietz, Denis de Freitas, Jan Corbet) delivered at Study Session in Antwerp, 1977, organised by Association Littéraire et Artistique Internationale and Association Belge pour la Protection du Droit d'Auteur.

Payment to Creators for Library Loans (Public Lending Right)/ Versement d'une Redevance Bibliothèque (Droit de Prêt Public). Document 4070. Recommmendation 822 (1977). Strasbourg, 1977: Council of Europe, Parliamentary Assembly.

Prices, Costs and Margins in the Publishing, Printing and Binding, and Distribution of Books. Price Commission. London, 1978: HMSO.

Public Lending Right. North Sydney, 1978: published for Public Lending Right by the Arts Information Program of the Australia Council.

Public Lending Right: An Account of an investigation of technical and cost aspects. Department of Education and Science. London, 1975: HMSO.

Public Lending Right: Final Report of an investigation of technical and cost aspects. Department of Education and Science. London, 1975: HMSO.

Reform of the Law relating to Copyright, Designs and Performers' Protection. A consultative document. Cmnd. 8302. London, 1981: HMSO.

Van geen recht naar leenrecht. Netherlands, 1975: Vereniging van Letterkundigen and Vakbond van Schrijvers.

Legislation

(Denmark)
The Danish Public Libraries Act 1964. Copenhagen, 1977: The State Inspection of Public Libraries.

(Germany)
National Legislation, Germany (Federal Republic). Act dealing with Copyright and Related Rights (Copyright Act) of September 9, 1965.

(United Kingdom)
Copyright Act, 1956. Chapter 74. An Act to make new provision in respect of copyright and related matters, in substitution for the provisions of the Copyright Act, 1911,

and other enactments relating thereto; to amend the Registered Designs Act, 1949, with respect to designs related to artistic works in which copyright subsists, and to amend the Dramatic and Musical Performers' Protection Act, 1925; and for purposes connected with the matters aforesaid. (5 November, 1956).

Public Libraries and Museums Act, 1964. Chapter 75. An Act to place the public library service provided by local authorities in England and Wales under the superintendence of the Secretary of State, to make new provision for regulating and improving that service and as to the provision and maintenance of museums and art galleries by such authorities, and for purposes connected with the matters aforesaid. (31 July 1964).

Appendix A

Public Lending Right Act 1979

CHAPTER 10

ARRANGEMENT OF SECTIONS

Public Lending Right Act 1979

1979 CHAPTER 10

An Act to provide public lending right for authors, and for connected purposes. [22nd March 1979]

BE IT ENACTED by the Queen's most Excellent Majesty, by and with the advice and consent of the Lords Spiritual and Temporal, and Commons, in this present Parliament assembled, and by the authority of the same, as follows:—

1.—(1) In accordance with a scheme to be prepared and brought into force by the Secretary of State, there shall be conferred on authors a right, known as " public lending right ", to receive from time to time out of a Central Fund payments in respect of such of their books as are lent out to the public by local library authorities in the United Kingdom. Establishmen of public lending right.

(2) The classes, descriptions and categories of books in respect of which public lending right subsists, and the scales of payments to be made from the Central Fund in respect of it, shall be determined by or in accordance with the scheme; and in preparing the scheme the Secretary of State shall consult with representatives of authors and library authorities and of others who appear to be likely to be affected by it.

(3) The Secretary of State shall appoint an officer to be known as the Registrar of Public Lending Right; and the Schedule to this Act has effect with respect to the Registrar.

(4) The Registrar shall be charged with the duty of establishing and maintaining in accordance with the scheme a register showing the books in respect of which public lending right subsists and the persons entitled to the right in respect of any registered book.

(5) The Registrar shall, in the case of any registered book determine in accordance with the scheme the sums (if any) due by way of public lending right; and any sum so determined to be due shall be recoverable from the Registrar as a debt due to the person for the time being entitled to that right in respect of the book.

(6) Subject to any provision made by the scheme, the duration of public lending right in respect of a book shall be from the date of the book's first publication (or, if later, the beginning of the year in which application is made for it to be registered) until 50 years have elapsed since the end of the year in which the author died.

(7) Provision shall be made by the scheme for the right—

    (a) to be established by registration;

    (b) to be transmissible by assignment or assignation, by testamentary disposition or by operation of law, as personal or moveable property;

    (c) to be claimed by or on behalf of the person for the time being entitled;

    (d) to be renounced (either in whole or in part, and either temporarily or for all time) on notice being given to the Registrar to that effect.

The Central Fund.

2.—(1) The Central Fund shall be constituted by the Secretary of State and placed under the control and management of the Registrar.

(2) There shall be paid into the Fund from time to time such sums, out of money provided by Parliament, as the Secretary of State with Treasury approval determines to be required for the purpose of satisfying the liabilities of the Fund; but in respect of the liabilities of any one financial year of the Fund the total of those sums shall not exceed £2 million less the total of any sums paid in that year, out of money so provided, under paragraph 2 of the Schedule to this Act (pay, pension, etc. of Registrar).

(3) With the consent of the Treasury, the Secretary of State may from time to time by order in a statutory instrument

increase the limit on the sums to be paid under subsection (2) above in respect of financial years beginning after that in which the order is made ; but no such order shall be made unless a draft of it has been laid before the House of Commons and approved by a resolution of that House.

(4) There shall be paid out of the Central Fund—

> (a) such sums as may in accordance with the scheme be due from time to time in respect of public lending right ; and

> (b) the administrative expenses of the Registrar and any other expenses and outgoings mentioned in this Act which are expressed to be payable from the Fund.

(5) Money received by the Registrar in respect of property disposed of, or otherwise in the course of his functions, or under this Act, shall be paid into the Central Fund, except in such cases as the Secretary of State otherwise directs with the approval of the Treasury ; and in any such case the money shall be paid into the Consolidated Fund.

(6) The Registrar shall keep proper accounts and other records and shall prepare in respect of each financial year of the Fund statements of account in such form as the Secretary of State may direct with Treasury approval ; and those statements shall, on or before 31st August next following the end of that year, be transmitted to the Comptroller and Auditor General, who shall examine and certify the statements and lay copies thereof, together with his report thereon, before each House of Parliament.

3.—(1) As soon as may be after this Act comes into force, The scheme the Secretary of State shall prepare the draft of a scheme for and its its purposes and lay a copy of the draft before each House of administratio Parliament.

(2) If the draft scheme is approved by a resolution of each House, the Secretary of State shall bring the scheme into force (in the form of the draft) by means of an order in a statutory instrument, to be laid before Parliament after it is made ; and the order may provide for different provisions of the scheme to come into force on different dates.

(3) The scheme shall be so framed as to make entitlement to public lending right dependent on, and its extent ascertainable by reference to, the number of occasions on which books are lent out from particular libraries, to be specified by the scheme or identified in accordance with provision made by it.

(4) For this purpose, " library "—

> (a) means any one of a local library authority's collections of books held by them for the purpose of being borrowed by the public ; and

(*b*) includes any such collection which is taken about from place to place.

(5) The scheme may provide for requiring local library authorities—

> (*a*) to give information as and when, and in the form in which, the Registrar may call for it or the Secretary of State may direct, as to loans made by them to the public of books in respect of which public lending right subsists, or of other books ; and

> (*b*) to arrange for books to be numbered, or otherwise marked or coded, with a view to facilitating the maintenance of the register and the ascertainment and administration of public lending right.

(6) The Registrar shall, by means of payments out of the Central Fund, reimburse to local library authorities any expenditure incurred by them in giving effect to the scheme, the amount of that expenditure being ascertained in accordance with such calculations as the scheme may prescribe.

(7) Subject to the provisions of this Act (and in particular to the foregoing provisions of this section), the scheme may be varied from time to time by the Secretary of State, after such consultation as is mentioned in section 1(2) above, and the variation brought into force by an order in a statutory instrument, subject to annulment in pursuance of a resolution of either House of Parliament ; and the variation may comprise such incidental and transitional provisions as the Secretary of State thinks appropriate for the purposes of continuing the scheme as varied.

(8) The Secretary of State shall in each year prepare and lay before each House of Parliament a report on the working of the scheme.

The register.   **4.**—(1) The register shall be kept in such form, and contain such particulars of books and their authors, as may be prescribed.

(2) No application for an entry in the register is to be entertained in the case of any book unless it falls within a class, description or category of books prescribed as one in respect of which public lending right subsists.

(3) The scheme shall provide for the register to be conclusive both as to whether public lending right subsists in respect of a particular book and also as to the persons (if any) who are for the time being entitled to the right.

(4) Provision shall be included in the scheme for entries in the register to be made and amended, on application made in the prescribed manner and supported by prescribed particulars (verified as prescribed) so as to indicate, in the case of any

book who (if any one) is for the time being entitled to public lending right in respect of it.

(5) The Registrar may direct the removal from the register of every entry relating to a book in whose case no sum has become due by way of public lending right for a period of at least 10 years, but without prejudice to a subsequent application for the entries to be restored to the register.

(6) The Registrar may require the payment of fees, according to prescribed scales and rates, for supplying copies of entries in the register ; and a copy of an entry, certified under the hand of the Registrar or an officer of his with authority in that behalf (which authority it shall be unnecessary to prove) shall in all legal proceedings be admissible in evidence as of equal validity with the original.

(7) It shall be an offence for any person, in connection with the entry of any matter whatsoever in the register, to make any statement which he knows to be false in a material particular or recklessly to make any statement which is false in a material particular ; and a person who commits an offence under this section shall be liable on summary conviction to a fine of not more than £1,000.

(8) Where an offence under subsection (7) above which has been committed by a body corporate is proved to have been committed with the consent or connivance of, or to be attributable to any neglect on the part of, a director, manager, secretary or other similar officer of the body corporate, or any person who was purporting to act in any such capacity, he (as well as the body corporate) shall be guilty of that offence and be liable to be proceeded against accordingly.

Where the affairs of a body corporate are managed by its members, this subsection applies in relation to the acts and defaults of a member in connection with his functions of management as if he were a director of the body corporate.

5.—(1) This Act may be cited as the Public Lending Right Citation, etc. Act 1979.

(2) In this Act any reference to " the scheme " is to the scheme prepared and brought into force by the Secretary of State in accordance with sections 1 and 3 of this Act (including the scheme as varied from time to time under section 3(7) ; and—

" local library authority " means—

(*a*) a library authority under the Public Libraries 1964 c. 75. and Museums Act 1964,

(*b*) a statutory library authority within the Public 1955 c. 27. Libraries (Scotland) Act 1955, and

S.I. 1972/1263
N.I. 12).

(c) an Education and Library Board within the Education and Libraries (Northern Ireland) Order 1972 ;

" prescribed " means prescribed by the scheme ;

" the register " means the register required by section 1(4) to be established and maintained by the Registrar ; and

" the Registrar " means the Registrar of Public Lending Right.

(3) This Act comes into force on a day to be appointed by an order made by the Secretary of State in a statutory instrument to be laid before Parliament after it has been made.

(4) This Act extends to Northern Ireland.

SCHEDULE

THE REGISTRAR OF PUBLIC LENDING RIGHT

1. The Registrar shall hold and vacate office as such in accordance with the terms of his appointment ; but he may at any time resign his office by notice in writing addressed to the Secretary of State ; and the Secretary of State may at any time remove a person from the office of Registrar on the ground of incapacity or misbehaviour.

2.—(1) There shall be paid to the Registrar out of money provided by Parliament such remuneration and allowances as the Secretary of State may determine with the approval of the Minister for the Civil Service.

(2) In the case of any such holder of the office of Registrar as may be determined by the Secretary of State with that approval, there shall be paid out of money so provided such pension, allowance or gratuity to or in respect of him, or such contributions or payments towards provision of such a pension, allowance or gratuity, as may be so determined.

3. If, when a person ceases to hold office as Registrar, it appears to the Secretary of State that there are special circumstances which make it right that he should receive compensation, there may (with the approval of the Minister for the Civil Service) be paid to him out of the Central Fund a sum by way of compensation of such amount as may be so determined.

4. In the House of Commons Disqualification Act 1975, in Part III of Schedule 1 (other disqualifying offices), the following shall be inserted at the appropriate place in alphabetical order— *1975 c. 24.*

" Registrar of Public Lending Right " ;

and the like insertion shall be made in Part III of Schedule 1 to the Northern Ireland Assembly Disqualification Act 1975. *1975 c. 25.*

5.—(1) The Registrar of Public Lending Right shall be by that name a corporation sole, with a corporate seal.

(2) He is not to be regarded as the servant or agent of the Crown.

6. The Documentary Evidence Act 1868 shall have effect as if the Registrar were included in the first column of the Schedule to that Act, as if the Registrar and any person authorised to act on his behalf were mentioned in the second column of that Schedule, and as if the regulations referred to in that Act included any documents issued by the Registrar or by any such person. *1868 c. 37*

7.—(1) The Registrar may appoint such assistant registrars and staff as he thinks fit, subject to the approval of the Secretary of State as to their numbers ; and their terms and conditions of service, and the remuneration and allowances payable to them, shall be such as the Registrar may determine.

(2) The Registrar may direct, in the case of persons appointed by him under this paragraph—

  (*a*) that there be paid to and in respect of them such pensions, allowances and gratuities as he may determine ;

  (*b*) that payments be made towards the provision for them of such pensions, allowances and gratuities as he may determine ; and

  (*c*) that schemes be provided and maintained (whether contributory or not) for the payment to and in respect of them of such pensions, allowances and gratuities as he may determine.

(3) Any money required for the payment of remuneration and allowances under this paragraph, and of pensions, allowances and gratuities, and otherwise for the purposes of sub-paragraph (2) above, shall be paid from the Central Fund.

(4) The approval of the Secretary of State and the Minister for the Civil Service shall be required for any directions or determination by the Registrar under this paragraph.

8. Anything authorised or required under this Act (except paragraph 7 of this Schedule), or by or under the scheme, to be done by the Registrar may be done by any assistant registrar or member of the Registrar's staff who is authorised generally or specially in that behalf in writing by the Registrar.

Appendix B

STATUTORY INSTRUMENTS

1982 No. 719

LIBRARIES

The Public Lending Right Scheme 1982 (Commencement) Order 1982

Made - - - -	17*th May* 1982
Laid before Parliament	1*st June* 1982
Coming into Operation	14*th June* 1982

In exercise of the powers conferred on me by section 3 (2) of the Public Lending Right Act 1979(**a**), I hereby make the following Order:—

1. This Order may be cited as the Public Lending Right Scheme 1982 (Commencement) Order 1982 and shall come into operation on 14th June 1982.

2.—(1) The Scheme set out in the Appendix hereto, which has been approved by a resolution of each House of Parliament, shall come into force in the manner hereinafter provided.

(2) The provisions of the Scheme specified in column 1 of the table set out below shall come into force on the dates specified in relation thereto in column 2 of that table:

(1) Provisions of the Scheme	(2) Date on which provisions come into force
Parts I, II and IV, Schedule 2 and Schedule 3 Part I	14th June 1982
Part III and Schedule 1	1st September 1982
Part V, Schedule 3 Part II and Schedule 4	1st July 1983

Keith Joseph,
Secretary of State for
Education and Science.

17th May 1982.

(**a**) 1979 c. 10.

APPENDIX

PUBLIC LENDING RIGHT SCHEME 1982

ARRANGEMENT OF SCHEME

PART I

TITLE AND INTERPRETATION

PART II

BOOKS AND AUTHORS ELIGIBLE UNDER THE SCHEME

PART III

REGISTRATION OF PUBLIC LENDING RIGHT

The Register

Procedure for Registration

First Registration

PART IV

ASCERTAINMENT OF THE NUMBER OF LOANS OF BOOKS

PART V

CALCULATION AND PAYMENT OF PUBLIC LENDING RIGHT

SCHEDULES

PUBLIC LENDING RIGHT SCHEME 1982

PART I

TITLE AND INTERPRETATION

Citation and extent

1. This Scheme may be cited as the Public Lending Right Scheme 1982, and shall extend to the whole of the United Kingdom.

General definitions

2.—(1) In this Scheme, except where the context otherwise requires, the following expressions have the meanings hereby respectively assigned to them, that is to say—

"the Act" means the Public Lending Right Act 1979(**a**);

"author", in relation to an eligible book, means a person who is, or one of a number of persons who are, treated as such by Article 4;

(**a**) 1979 c. 10.

"eligible author", in relation to an eligible book, means an author of that book who is an eligible person;

"eligible book" has the meaning assigned thereto by Article 6;

"eligible person", in relation to an author, has the meaning assigned thereto by Article 5;

"financial year" means a period of twelve months ending on the 31st March;

"identifying number" means the number entered in the Register in pursuance of Article 8(1)(a)(iv);

"library" means any one of a local library authority's collections of books held by them for the purpose of being borrowed by the public, but does not include any such collection which is taken about from place to place;

"local library authority" has the meaning assigned thereto by section 5(2) of the Act;

"the Registrar" and "the Register" have the meanings assigned thereto by section 5(2) of the Act;

"registered interest" means the interest (being the whole or a share thereof), in the Public Lending Right in respect of a particular book, shown on the Register as belonging to a particular person, and "registered owner" means the person for the time being so registered;

"the registry" means the place at which the Register is for the time being maintained in pursuance of Article 7;

"sampling year" has the meaning assigned thereto by Article 36.

(2) In this Scheme, except where the context otherwise requires, any reference to an Article or to a Part or to a Schedule shall be construed as a reference to an Article contained in, or to a Part of or a Schedule to, this Scheme, as the case may be, and any reference in any Article to a paragraph shall be construed as a reference to a paragraph in that Article.

Delivery of documents and service of notice

3. Unless the context otherwise requires, any requirement in this Scheme for—

(a) a document or an application to be delivered at the registry or produced to the Registrar or for notice to be given to him, shall be satisfied if the same is either—

    (i) delivered in person at the registry between the hours of 11 am and 3pm on a working day; or

    (ii) sent through the post by recorded delivery;

(b) a local library authority or a registered owner to be notified of any matter shall be satisfied if such notification is sent through the post.

PART II

BOOKS AND AUTHORS ELIGIBLE UNDER THE SCHEME

Authors

4.—(1) Subject to paragraph (2), for the purpose of this Scheme a person shall be treated as an author of a book if he is either—

(a) a writer of the book; or

(b) an illustrator thereof, which for this purpose includes the author of a photograph (within the meaning of section 48 of the Copyright Act 1956(**a**)).

(2) Notwithstanding paragraph (1), a person shall not be treated as an author of a book—

(a) unless the fact that he is an author within the meaning of paragraph (1) is evidenced by his being named on the title page of the book; or

(b) if the nature of his contribution thereto is that of an editor, compiler,. reviser or translator.

Eligible persons

5.—(1) For the purposes of the Scheme, and in relation to each application by a person relating to an eligible book, he is an eligible person if he is an author (within the meaning of Article 4) of that book who—

(a) is a British citizen or, if not such a citizen (by reason that the British Nationality Act 1981(**b**) is not in force or otherwise), is a national of the United Kingdom or of any other member state of the European Economic Community (as for the time being constituted) for the purposes of the Community Treaties; and

(b) at the date of the application has his only or principal home in the United Kingdom, or, if he has no home, has been present in the United Kingdom for not less than twelve months out of the preceding twenty-four months.

(2) In this Article, "principal home", in the case of a person having more than one home means that one of those homes at which he has been for the longest aggregate period during the twenty-four months immediately preceding the application for registration.

Eligible books

6.—(1) For the purposes of this Scheme, an eligible book is a book (as defined in paragraph (2)) the sole author, or at least one of the authors, of which is an eligible person; and there shall be treated as a separate book—

(**a**) 1956 c. 74.   (**b**) 1981 c. 61.

(a) each volume of a work published in two or more volumes, and

(b) each new edition of a book.

(2) In paragraph (1) "book" means a printed and bound publication (including a paper-back edition) containing not less than 32 such pages of printed text as are mentioned in paragraph (3), or not less than 24 such pages where at least a half of them are pages of poetry or drama:

Provided that "book" does not include—

(a) a book bearing, in lieu of the name of an author who is a natural person, the name of a body corporate or an unincorporated association;

(b) a book with four or more authors or, in the case of an encyclopaedia, dictionary or comparable publication, with two or more authors;

(c) a book the copyright in which is vested in the Crown;

(d) a book which has not been offered for sale to the public, or

(e) a serial publication including, without prejudice to the generality of that expression, a newspaper, magazine, journal or periodical.

(3) The pages of printed text referred to in paragraph (2) are pages, other than end papers, of which not less than a half of the area of each page (excluding margins) is occupied by print otherwise than by way of a printed illustration.

PART III

REGISTRATION OF PUBLIC LENDING RIGHT

The Register

The Register

7. The Registrar shall establish and maintain a Public Lending Right Register at such place as the Secretary of State may from time to time determine, and upon each such determination notice shall be published in the London Gazette, the Edinburgh Gazette and the Belfast Gazette, of such place and the time of the commencement of registration thereat.

The content of the Register

8.—(1) The Register shall contain—

(a) particulars of each book in respect of which Public Lending Right subsists, including—

   (i) the title of the book;

   (ii) the name or names of the persons appearing on the title page as the authors thereof;

   (iii) the true identity of an author if different from (ii) above;

    (iv) a number for that book, determined by, or in accordance with arrangements made by, the Registrar;

  (b) the name and address of each person entitled to the Right in respect of each such book and, if more than one, the share of each such person in such Right.

(2) The Registrar shall also keep at the registry an index whereby all entries in the Register can readily be traced, and for this purpose "index" includes any device or combination of devices serving the purpose of an index.

Registration

9.—(1) Public Lending Right in respect of a book may, and may only, be registered if—

  (a) the book is an eligible book, and

  (b) the author thereof, or if the book has two or more authors, all the authors thereof (including any who are not eligible persons) are alive at the date of the application for first registration of the Right,

and application in that behalf is made in accordance with Articles 14 and 17.

(2) Subject to paragraph (3), an eligible author's share of the Public Lending Right in respect of an eligible book with two or more authors (including any who are not eligible persons) may, and may only, be registered on application in that behalf made as aforesaid.

(3) The share of the Public Lending Right in such a book as is mentioned in paragraph (2) of an author who was not an eligible person at the time when application was first made for the registration of the share of the Right of any co-author may, and may only, be registered if—

  (a) he has become and remains an eligible person, and

  (b) all the authors of the book (including any who are not eligible persons) are alive at the date of his application for registration of his share,

and application in that behalf is made as aforesaid.

Dealings to be effected only on the Register

10. No Public Lending Right in respect of a particular book shall subsist and no transmission of a registered interest shall be effective until such Right or such transmission has been entered in the Register by the Registrar.

Register to be conclusive

11. The Register shall be conclusive as to whether Public Lending Right subsists in respect of a particular book and also as to the persons (if any) who are for the time being entitled to the Right.

Amendment of the Register

12. The Register may be amended pursuant to an Order of a Court of competent jurisdiction or by the decision of the Registrar in any of the following cases—

(a) in any case and at any time with the consent of the registered owner or owners of the Right in respect of a particular book;

(b) where a Court of competent jurisdiction or the Registrar is satisfied that an entry in the Register has been obtained by fraud;

(c) where a decision of a Court of competent jurisdiction affects any interest in an eligible book and, in consequence thereof, the Registrar is of the opinion that amendment of the Register is required;

(d) where two or more persons are erroneously registered as being entitled to the same interest in Public Lending Right in respect of a particular book;

(e) where an entry erroneously relates to a book which is not an eligible book;

(f) in any other case where by reason of any error or omission in the Register, or by reason of any entry made under a mistake, it appears to the Registrar just to amend the Register.

Payments consequent upon amendment

13. The person who, as a result of an amendment of the Register pursuant to Article 12 becomes the registered owner of a registered interest shall be entitled to the payment of Public Lending Right in respect of that interest from the date upon which the Register was amended.

Procedure for Registration

Forms of application

14. Any application required under this Scheme—

(a) for first registration of Public Lending Right or of an eligible author's share of the Right;

(b) for the transfer of a registered interest, or

(c) for renunciation of a registered interest,

shall be made in writing to the Registrar and provide the information specified in Part I, II or III of Schedule 1 (as the case may be) in such form as he may from time to time require.

Recording of receipt of application

15. The Registrar shall record the date upon which each application for first registration is received by him.

Completion of registration

16.—(1) When the Registrar is satisfied as to the eligibility of a book for registration and as to the persons entitled to Public Lending Right in respect of that book and, if more than one, of their respective shares therein, the registration shall be completed and, as regards a first registration of the Right, each registration shall be effective as from the day the application was recorded by the Registrar as having been received by him.

(2) On completion of a registration the Registrar shall issue to any person so entered in the Register as having an interest in the Public Lending Right in respect of the book to which the entry relates, an acknowledgement of registration in the form of a copy of the relevant entry, indicating therein the date from which the entry takes effect.

First Registration

Application for first registration

17.—(1) An application for first registration of Public Lending Right in respect of an eligible book—

(a) shall satisfy the requirements of Article 14 and be made by delivery at the registry;

(b) shall be made by an eligible author, and

(c) where the book has two or more authors (including any who are not eligible persons), shall specify the shares of each of them in the Right and, for that purpose, each of those authors shall be a party to the application.

(2) An application for first registration of an eligible author's share of Public Lending Right in respect of an eligible book with two or more authors (including any who are not eligible persons)—

(a) shall satisfy the requirements of Article 14 and be made by delivery at the registry, and

(b) shall be made by the author concerned.

(3) Anything which falls to be done by an author under this Article shall, if he is not of full age, be done by his parent or guardian and that parent or guardian shall be recorded in the Register as the person to whom are payable sums in respect of any registered interest of the author until such time as a transfer of the registration into the author's own name has been recorded in pursuance of Article 25.

Evidence required in connection with the applications

18. The Registrar may require the submission of evidence to satisfy him that a book is an eligible book and that a person applying as author for the first registration of Public Lending Right, or the registration of a share of the Right, in respect thereof—

154

(a) is in fact the author of that book;

(b) is an eligible person;

but for the purposes hereof he shall be entitled to rely upon a statutory declaration or a declaration made before a Notary Public.

Subsequent dealings with Public Lending Right

Public Lending Right to be transmissible

19. A registered interest shall be transmissible by assignment or assignation, by testamentary disposition or by operation of law, as personal or movable property, so long, as regards a particular book, as the Right in respect of that book is capable of subsisting.

Period during which the Right may be transferred

20. The duration of Public Lending Right in respect of any book and the period during which there may be dealings therein shall be from the date of the book's first publication (or, if later, the beginning of the sampling year in which application is made for it to be registered) until fifty years have elapsed since the end of the sampling year in which the author died or, if the book is registered as the work of more than one author, as regards dealings in the share of the Right attributable to that author, the end of the year in which that author died.

Whole interest to be assigned

21.—(1) The disposition of Public Lending Right, after the first registration thereof, shall, as respects each registered interest in any book, be for the whole of that interest.

(2) On such disposition the interest may be registered in the name of joint owners, being not more than four in number and all being of full age, but in such case the senior only shall be deemed, for the purposes of the Scheme, to be the registered owner; seniority shall be determined by the order in which names stand in the Register.

(3) Subject to Articles 29 and 30, no notice of any trusts, expressed, implied or constructive, shall be entered on the Register or be receivable by the Registrar.

Applications for transfer

22. Every application for registration of a transfer of Public Lending Right shall satisfy the requirements of Article 14 and be made by delivery at the registry.

Stamp duty

23.—(1) An application for transfer shall bear the proper Inland Revenue stamp impressed thereon to show that all duty payable (if any) in respect of the transaction has been paid.

(2) Where an application for transfer is submitted for the purpose of giving effect to a transaction under a deed or other instrument on which the Inland Revenue stamp has already been impressed, such stamped instrument shall,

before completion of the registration, be produced to the Registrar to show that all duty payable (if any) in respect of the transaction has been paid.

Proof of author's existence

24. It shall be a condition of registration of every transfer that the transferee provides, and gives an undertaking to the Registrar in future to provide at such intervals and in such form as the Registrar may require, evidence that the author is still alive, or, as the case may be, evidence of the author's death.

Registration by an author on attainment of full age

25. An author whose interest is, pursuant to Article 17(3), registered in the name of his parent or guardian may, on attaining full age, make application to the Registrar in accordance with Articles 21 to 23, so far as they are applicable, for the transfer of the registration of the Right into his own name, and until such transfer has been recorded the Registrar shall be entitled to remit any sums due in respect of the Right to such parent or guardian.

Transmission on death

Registration of personal representatives

26. On production of the probate, letters of administration, or confirmation of executors of a registered owner, the personal representatives named in such probate, letters or confirmation shall, on production of the same to the Registrar, be registered as owner in place of the deceased owner with the addition of the words "executor *or* executrix (*or* administrator *or* administratrix) of *[name]* deceased".

Transfer by personal representatives

27. The personal representatives registered under the preceding Article may transfer the interest of the deceased owner, such transfer being in accordance with Articles 21 to 24 or such provisions thereof as are applicable in the circumstances of the case.

Transfer on bankruptcy, liquidation or sequestration

Registration of Official Receiver, Official Assignees or Judicial Factor

28.—(1) On the production to the Registrar of an office copy of an Order of a Court having jurisdiction in bankruptcy adjudging a registered owner bankrupt or directing the estate of a deceased registered owner to be administered under section 130 of the Bankruptcy Act 1914(a) or section 21 of the Bankruptcy Amendment Act (Northern Ireland) 1929(b), together with a

---

(a) 1914 c. 59.   (b) 1929 c. 1 (N.I.).

certificate signed by the Official Receiver or Official Assignee, as the case may be, that any registered interest in the name of the bankrupt registered owner, or deceased registered owner, is part of his property divisible amongst his creditors, the Official Receiver or the Official Assignee may be registered as the registered owner in place of the bankrupt or deceased registered owner.

(2) Where there is produced to the Registrar a certified copy of an Order of a Court having competent jurisdiction in Scotland awarding sequestration of the estate of a registered owner (including a deceased registered owner) and appointing a judicial factor the Registrar shall on receipt of such a copy enter in the Register the name of the judicial factor as registered owner with the addition of the words "judicial factor in the estate of *[name]*".

Registration of Trustee in Bankruptcy in place of Official Receiver, Assignees in Bankruptcy or Judicial Factor

29.—(1) Where the Official Receiver or the Official Assignee has been registered as registered owner and some other person is subsequently appointed trustee, or, in Northern Ireland, a creditor's assignee is appointed, the trustee or the assignee may be registered as registered owner in place of the Official Receiver, or the Official Assignee, on production of an office copy of the certificate by the Department of Trade of his appointment as trustee, or in Northern Ireland an office copy of the certificate under section 90 of the Bankruptcy (Ireland) Amendment Act 1872(a) or of the certificate of the vesting of the estate and effects of the registered owner in the assignee.

(2) Where a judicial factor has been registered as an owner in terms of Article 28(2) and some other person is subsequently elected as a trustee for behoof of the creditors of the former registered owner, the Registrar, on receipt of the notification of such election and of sufficient evidence to demonstrate that that person has been so elected, shall enter in the Register the name of the trustee as registered owner with the addition of the words "trustee in the estate of *[name]*".

(3) If the Official Receiver or the Official Assignee has not been entered on the Register under Article 28 (1) the trustee or the assignee may be registered as registered owner on production of office copies of the Order adjudging the registered owner bankrupt and the appropriate certificate referred to in paragraph (1) with a certificate signed by the trustee or the assignee that the registered interest is part of the property of the bankrupt divisible amongst his creditors.

(4) If a judicial factor has not been entered in the Register as owner under Article 28(2) the Registrar shall, on receipt of the certified copy of an Order of a Court under Article 28(2) together with the notification and evidence referred to in paragraph (2), enter in the Register as registered owner the name of the duly elected trustee with the addition of the words "trustee in the estate of *[name]*".

(a) 1872 c. 58.

Registration of a trust under a Scheme of Arrangement or an Arrangement under the control of the Court

30.—(1) If any registered interest is vested in a trustee under the provisions of a Scheme of Arrangement approved by a Court having jurisdiction in bankruptcy, the Official Receiver or other trustee may be registered as owner in like manner as a trustee in bankruptcy upon production of an office copy of the Scheme of Arrangement, a certificate signed by the Official Receiver, or such other trustee, that the registered interest was part of the property vested in him under the provisions of the Scheme, and in the case of a trustee other than the Official Receiver, an office copy of the certificate by the Department of Trade of his appointment as trustee.

(2) If any registered interest of an arranging debtor who is a registered owner is vested in the Official Assignee alone or jointly with other persons under section 349 of the Irish Bankrupt and Insolvent Act 1857(a), the Official Assignee and such other persons (if any) may be registered as owner in his place on production of an office copy of the Order of the Court approving and confirming the resolution or agreement referred to in the said section with a certificate by the Official Assignee identifying the arranging debtor named in the Order of the Court with the registered owner endorsed thereon and a certificate signed by the Official Assignee and other such person (if any) that the registered interest was part of the property vested under the resolution or agreement.

(3) If, as regards Scotland, a registered owner—

(a) has entered into a deed of arrangement for behoof of his creditors, the Registrar shall, on receiving a certified copy of the Order of the Court approving such arrangement, enter on the Register as owner the name of the person who is under the said deed of arrangement to receive any payments due to the owner (where that person is not the registered owner at the date of approval of the arrangement);

(b) has entered into a private trust deed or composition contract for behoof of his creditors, the trustee under such deed or contract may make an application, accompanied by such evidence as the Registrar may require, for transmission of the registered interest into his name as such trustee; and on receipt of such an application the Registrar shall make the appropriate entry in the Register.

Liquidation of a company

31. In the liquidation of a company in which an interest in Public Lending Right is vested, any resolution or order appointing a liquidator may be filed and referred to on the Register, and, when so registered, shall be deemed to be in force until it is cancelled or superseded on the Register.

(a) 1857 c. 60.

Renunciation

32.—(1) On making application in that behalf which satisfies the requirements of Article 14, the registered owner of a registered interest may absolutely and unconditionally renounce that interest as provided in paragraph (2).

(2) Such renunciation may, as to extent, be in respect of either the whole or a half share of the registered interest and may be effective for all time, or in respect of such financial years as shall be specified by the registered owner.

(3) An application for renunciation shall bear the proper Inland Revenue stamp impressed thereon.

(4) The Registrar shall as at the date from which the renunciation is to have effect amend the Register—

(a) in the case of a renunciation for all time of the whole of the registered interest by removing from the Register the entry relating to the registered owner and, if that interest represents the whole of the Public Lending Right in a book, the entry relating to that book; or

(b) in all other cases, by noting against the relevant entry in the Register the extent of the renunciation and the period during which it is effective.

(5) Immediately upon the amendment of the Register as provided in paragraph (4), any sum due by way of Public Lending Right which, apart from the renunciation would become payable to the registered owner by 31st March in any year falling within the period to which the renunciation applies, shall cease to be so payable.

General

Neglected applications for registration

33. Where in the case of any application for first or any subsequent registration an applicant has failed to provide within three months information requested by the Registrar, notice may be given to the applicant that the application will be treated as abandoned unless the information is duly furnished within a time (not being less than one month) determined by the Registrar and specified in the notice; and if, at the expiration of that time, the information so requested is not furnished, the application may be treated as abandoned.

Removal of entries from the Register

34. Where the Registrar, pursuant to section 4(5) of the Act, directs the removal from the Register of any entry relating to a book in whose case no sum has become due by way of Public Lending Right for a period of at least ten years, any subsequent application for the entry to be restored to the Register may be made only by the person who, at the date of the removal of the entry, was the registered owner, or by his legal personal representatives.

Copies of entries in the Register

35.—(1) The Registrar shall not supply a copy of any entry in the Register otherwise than to—

(a) a registered owner, as regards any entry which relates to his registered interest; or

(b) such other person as the registered owner may direct, but if the entry in question also relates to other registered owners, only with the consent of all such owners.

(2) The Registrar may require a payment of a fee for supplying a copy of an entry in the Register, not exceeding £5 in respect of each such entry.

PART IV

ASCERTAINMENT OF THE NUMBER OF LOANS OF BOOKS

Special definitions

36. In this Part, unless the context otherwise requires—

"copy" means an individual copy of a particular book, and "copy number" means a number which distinguishes the copy to which it is applied from other copies of the same book in the same library;

"group", in relation to service points, means a group specified in Schedule 2;

"loans" means loans whereby books are lent out from a service point to individual borrowers, and includes loans of books not normally held at that service point;

"month" means one of the twelve months in the calendar year;

"operative sampling point" means a sampling point at which loans are for the time being required to be recorded in pursuance of Article 40(1);

"ordinary service point" means a service point from which fewer than 500,000 loans were made during the preceding period of twelve months;

"participating period", in relation to a sampling point, means the period commencing on the date on which the local library authority having responsibility for it receives from the Registrar notice of designation pursuant to Article 38(6) and ending on the date specified in a notice given thereunder as the date upon which it is to cease to act as a sampling point;

"principal service point", in relation to a library authority, means any of the following—

(a) whichever of the service points for which that authority is responsible is the service point from which the greatest number of loans were made during the preceding period of twelve months;

(b) any service point for which that authority is responsible, the number of loans from which during the preceding period of twelve months was not less than three-quarters of the number of loans made from the service point referred to in sub-paragraph (a) during the same period;

(c) any other such service point from which 500,000 or more loans were made during the aforesaid period;

and "principal service points" means every service point which is a principal service point in relation to any library authority;

"sampling point" means any principal service point or ordinary service point which has been designated, for the time being, by the Registrar under Article 38;

"sampling year" means the period of twelve months ending on 30th June;

"service point" means a place from which books comprised in a library are lent out to the public at large.

Number of loans to be ascertained by means of a sample

37. The number of occasions on which a book is lent out shall be determined by means of a sample of the lendings of that book from particular service points, designated in accordance with the provisions of this Part; and for the purpose of the sample, service points shall be classified into the groups, according to local library authority areas, specified in Schedule 2.

Designation of sampling points

38.—(1) Such local library authorities as the Registrar may require shall, not later than 30th September in each year, furnish to the Registrar lists, as at 31st March of that year, of all their ordinary service points and all their principal service points, and the Registrar shall, not later than 31st December of that year, designate in accordance with paragraph (6) those service points which are to be operative sampling points as from the beginning of the ensuing sampling year.

(2) The Registrar shall so exercise his powers under this Article as to secure, subject to paragraph (4), that—

(a) at all times there shall be 16 operative sampling points comprising—

(i) 3 points falling within each of Groups A and B in Schedule 2, in each case, subject to paragraph (3), including a principal service point and an ordinary service point, and

(ii) 2 points falling within each of the other groups, subject to paragraph (3), being a principal service point and an ordinary service point respectively;

(b) at all times one of the 2 operative sampling points falling within Group E in Schedule 2 shall be within either the county of Dyfed or that of Gwynedd;

(c) with effect from the beginning of each sampling year, 4 out of the 16 operative sampling points shall be replaced by new such points, and

(d) no service point remains an operative sampling point for a continuous period of more than four years.

(3) The relevant local library authority shall notify the Registrar of any change in the categorisation of a sampling point as a principal or ordinary service point but the Registrar shall not be required by paragraph (2)(a) to discontinue the designation of the point as a sampling point before the expiry of the sampling year in which he receives such notice or, if that year has less than six months to run, before the expiry of the next following sampling year.

For the purposes of this paragraph and of paragraph (2)(a), a change in the categorisation of a sampling point shall be disregarded if it is occasioned by an increase or decrease of less than 10% in the number of loans made therefrom.

(4) The local library authority shall notify the Registrar of any decision to close a sampling point and the date on which the closure takes effect but, if it is not reasonably practicable for the Registrar to satisfy the requirements of paragraph (2) before the closure takes effect, those requirements shall be treated as satisfied if satisfied as soon as is reasonably practicable thereafter.

(5) If it appears to the Registrar that an accurate sample would thereby be obtained more effectively, he may with effect from the beginning of the next sampling year, replace an existing sampling point by a new point, by designating such new sampling point in accordance with paragraphs (2) and (6), and by notifying the local library authority responsible that the existing sampling point is to be discontinued.

(6) The Registrar shall give to the local library authority responsible for a sampling point—

(a) for the purposes of designating that point under paragraph (1), notice in writing of such designation specifying the period he intends the point to be an operative sampling point;

(b) for the purpose of discontinuing that point as a sampling point, not less than six months notice in writing of such discontinuance.

Provision by libraries of recording facilities

39. Upon receipt of a notice under Article 38(6)(a) a local library authority shall—

(a) arrange for every book which may be lent out from the sampling point to which the designation refers to be marked, in such form as the Registrar may require, with its identifying number and (where more than one copy may be lent out) copy number, and shall notify the Registrar at such time and in such manner as he may direct of the number of books so marked; and

(b) acquire, in accordance with arrangements approved by the Registrar, such equipment (including computer programs) as may be necessary to enable the authority to comply with the provision of Article 40 regarding the furnishing of information to the Registrar.

Duty to record lendings

40.—(1) A local library authority which has received a notice under Article 38(6)(a) shall, for such period as is specified in the notice, record every occasion on which a copy of a book is lent out to the public from the sampling point to which the notice refers and shall furnish to the Registrar, in such form and at such intervals as he may direct, details of such lendings, including the identifying number and any copy number of the copy in question.

(2) For the purpose of this Article each volume of a work published in two or more volumes shall be treated as a separate book.

Provision of book loan data

41. Each local library authority shall submit to the Registrar, in such form, at such intervals and in respect of such periods as he may direct, a return of the total number of occasions on which the books comprised in all its collections were the subject of loans.

Method of determining the number of notional loans

42.—(1) The Registrar shall, from the details of loans furnished to him by local library authorities pursuant to the provisions of this Part (upon the accuracy of which the Registrar shall be entitled to rely), calculate, in accordance with paragraph (2), the number of notional loans of each book in respect of which Public Lending Right subsists in each sampling year.

(2) The number of notional loans of each book made during a sampling year shall be the aggregate of the number of notional loans of that book made in all groups; and the number of notional loans for a group shall be determined in accordance with the following formula:—

$$\text{Total notional loans in the group} = \frac{A}{B} \times C$$

Where—

A represents the number of loans of that book recorded during the sampling year at the operative sampling points in that group;

B represents the total number of loans of books made to the public during the sampling year from the operative sampling points in that group; and

C represents the aggregate of the loans of all books made to the public from all libraries (within the meaning of section 3(4) of the Act) in the area of the group during the financial year ending in the sampling year in question, or, as regards any particular library for which loan data relating to that financial year is not available to the Registrar, the most recent financial year for which he has such data.

163

(3) For the purposes of paragraph (2) any loans of a copy of a book at a particular sampling point in excess of twelve within a month shall be disregarded.

Reimbursement of local library authorities

43.—(1) The Registrar shall, subject to the provisions of this Article and Article 44, reimburse to local library authorities the net expenditure incurred by them in giving effect to this Scheme.

(2) It shall be the duty of local library authorities to keep proper accounts and records in respect of the expenditure (including overhead expenses) incurred by them in giving effect to this Scheme and the Registrar may withhold payment to a local library authority, in whole or in part, until such time as such authority has furnished to him sufficient evidence as to the amount of the expenditure so incurred.

Expense incurred in respect of sampling points

44.—(1) Without prejudice to the generality of Article 43(2) each local library authority to which a notice has been given under Article 38(6)(a) shall submit to the Registrar at such time and in such form as he may require estimates of the net expenditure to be incurred in giving effect to this Scheme at the sampling point or points specified in such notice.

(2) Such local library authority may from time to time during the participating period submit to the Registrar claims in respect of the expenditure incurred, or estimated to have been incurred by it, and the Registrar shall be entitled to rely upon the accuracy of such claims and to make payments on account of the expenditure incurred by that authority in giving effect to the Scheme.

(3) The total amount payable by way of reimbursement to such local library authority shall be finally determined by the Registrar after examination of such audited financial statements and such books, records, documents, and accounts relating thereto as he may require; and any balance found after such final determination to be due by or to the Registrar in account with the local library authority in question shall be paid to or recovered from such local library authority.

(4) In reckoning the net expenditure for the purposes of this Article and of Article 43, the following shall be deducted from the gross expenditure incurred by a local library authority in connection with a sampling point—

(a) any sum received in connection with the disposal (by sale, lease or otherwise) of any property or equipment purchased pursuant to sub-paragraph (b) of Article 39;

(b) any sum which it might reasonably be expected would have been received on such a disposal (whether or not there has been a disposal of the property or equipment in question);

(c) any insurance monies received in respect of the loss or destruction of or damage to any such property or equipment;

(d) an amount representing the appropriate proportion of the net cost (whether by way of purchase, lease, or otherwise) of any property or equipment which is used by a local library authority partly in connection with this Scheme and partly for other purposes not connected therewith:

Provided that where deductions are made under both sub-paragraphs (a) and (b) in respect of the same property or equipment, the aggregate deductions thereunder shall not exceed whichever is the greater of the sums mentioned in those sub-paragraphs.

(5) In determining the amount finally to be paid to or recovered from a local library authority pursuant to paragraph (3), account shall be taken of any expenditure reasonably incurred by that authority in discontinuing the sampling point.

Establishment of initial sample

45. The provisions set out in Part I of Schedule 3 shall have effect for the purpose of establishing the initial sampling points under this Scheme.

PART V

CALCULATION AND PAYMENT OF PUBLIC LENDING RIGHT

Determination of the sum due in respect of Public Lending Right

46.—(1) For any financial year, the sum due by way of Public Lending Right in respect of a registered interest to the registered owner thereof shall be ascertained by reference to—

(a) the product of the number of notional loans attributable to that interest (calculated in accordance with paragraph (4)) and 0·5p, and

(b) the aggregate amount of that product and the like products in the case of all other registered interests which initially were registered interests of the same author.

(2) Subject to paragraph (3) the sum so due for the financial year shall be—

(a) except where the following sub-paragraph applies, the product mentioned in paragraph (1)(a);

(b) if the aggregate amount mentioned in paragraph (1)(b) exceeds £5,000, the product of $\frac{x}{y}$ and £5,000 where—

x is the number of notional loans attributable to the interest in question, and

y is the aggregate of that number and the number of notional loans attributable to all other registered interests which initially were registered interests of the same author.

(3) If the amount determined in accordance with paragraph (2) is less than £5, the sum due in respect of the registered interest shall be nil.

(4) For the purposes of paragraphs (1) and (2) (b), the number of notional loans attributable to any registered interest in any financial year shall be calculated by ascertaining, in accordance with Article 42(2), the number of notional loans of the book to which it relates which were made during the sampling year ending in that financial year, and shall be—

(a) if the registered interest represents the whole of the Public Lending Right in respect of that book, the total notional loans of the book in question;

(b) if the registered interest relates only to a share of the Public Lending Right in respect of that book, such proportion of the total notional loans of the book as the registered interest bears to the whole of the Public Lending Right in that book, fractions of a loan being disregarded;

(c) if the Right in respect of that registered interest has been renounced in part, such proportion of the notional loans attributable to the registered interest under sub-paragraph (a) or (b), as the case may be, which the unrenounced share bears to the whole of the registered interest, fractions of a loan being disregarded;

(d) nil, if the Right in respect of the registered interest has been wholly renounced for the financial year in question.

(5) For the purposes of paragraphs (1) and (2)(b), the references to interests which were initially registered interests of the same author include interests which, in pursuance of Article 17(3), were registered in the name of his parent or guardian.

Persons to whom the payment is due

47. The person entitled to the Public Lending Right in respect of any registered book in any financial year shall be the registered owner thereof as at 30th June of that year.

Right to be claimed

48.—(1) No payment shall be made in respect of Public Lending Right unless that Right has been claimed by or on behalf of the person for the time being entitled.

(2) A claim in respect of the Right may be made for—

(a) a specified period;

(b) an unspecified period determinable by not less than three months written notice of termination given to the Registrar by or on behalf of the person for the time being entitled to the Right.

(3) A claim shall automatically lapse in the event of any change of ownership recorded on the Register, subsequent to first registration thereof, in respect of the Right to which the claim relates.

Notification of entitlement and payment of sums due under the Scheme

49.—(1) Any sum payable by way of Public Lending Right in respect of a registered interest, for any financial year, shall (unless sooner paid) fall due for payment on the last day of that year.

(2) Any such sum may be paid by cheque or warrant sent through the post directed to the registered address of the registered owner or, in the case of joint owners, to the registered address of the senior owner (as defined in Article 21(2)), or to such person and to such address as the owner or joint owners may direct by a written payment mandate to the Registrar, delivered at the registry, in the form set out in Schedule 4 or a form to the like effect; every such cheque or warrant shall be made payable to the order of the person to whom it is sent and any one of two or more joint owners may give a good receipt for any money due to them under this Scheme.

(3) The Registrar shall at the end of each financial year, or as soon as is reasonably practicable thereafter, inform each registered owner, by notice posted to his registered address of—

(a) the notional number of lendings for that year of each book in respect of which he is a registered owner; and

(b) the sum, if any, payable to him by way of Public Lending Right for each such book for the year in question.

(4) If, after the Registrar has notified the registered owner as provided in paragraph (3), the cheque or warrant for the sum referred to therein is not presented for payment and thereby lapses—

(a) there shall be no further duty on the part of the Registrar to take steps to trace the registered owner and it shall be the responsibility of such owner to make application to the Registrar for payment; and

(b) if at the end of six years from the date upon which a payment in respect of Public Lending Right becomes due no such application has been made by the person entitled thereto, the entitlement to such payment shall lapse.

Power to call for information

50. The Registrar may at any time require a statutory declaration or other sufficient evidence that an author or any registered owner is alive and is the person to whom money is payable under this Scheme, and may withhold payment until such declaration or evidence as he may require is produced.

Interest

51. No sum determined to be due under this Scheme shall carry interest.

Initial payment to authors

52. The provisions of Part II of Schedule 3 shall have effect for the purpose of determining the first sums payable in respect of Public Lending Right under this Scheme.

Article 14

SCHEDULE 1

INFORMATION TO BE PROVIDED IN CONNECTION WITH APPLICATIONS

PART I

APPLICATION FOR FIRST REGISTRATION

Each application shall provide the Registrar, in such form as he may from time to time require, with the following—

1. The title of the book to which the application relates.

2. The name of every person named on the title page as author (within the meaning of Article 4).

3. The true identity (if different from 2 above) of each such person, and his address.

4. The International Standard Book Number (if any) of the book.

5. A statutory declaration or a declaration made before a Notary Public (in respect of each applicant if more than one) deposing to the fact that (in each case) the conditions as to eligibility specified in Part II of the Scheme are satisfied at the date of application.

6. In the case of a work by more than one author, a joint declaration by all the authors as to their respective shares of the Public Lending Right.

7. In the case of an author not of full age, a declaration by the applicant that he is the parent or guardian, as the case may be, of the author, and a copy of the author's birth certificate.

PART II

APPLICATION FOR TRANSFER OF REGISTERED INTEREST

Each application shall provide the Registrar, in such form as he may from time to time require, with the following—

1. The title of the book.

2. The International Standard Book Number (if any) of the book.

3. The name and address of the transferor.

4. The name and address of the transferee.

5. An undertaking by the transferee to furnish to the Registrar, whenever so required, proof that the author is still alive.

PART III

APPLICATION FOR RENUNCIATION OF REGISTERED INTEREST

Each application shall provide the Registrar, in such form as he may from time to time require, with the following—

1. The name and address of the person renouncing.

2. The title of the book to which the renunciation relates.

3. The International Standard Book Number (if any) of the book.

4. The extent of the Right being renounced.

5. The period in respect of which the Right is renounced.

Articles 36–38   SCHEDULE 2

GROUPING OF SERVICE POINTS

Service points shall be grouped according to local library authority areas as follows—

GROUP A

Those within the areas of the following non-metropolitan counties—

Cheshire	Humberside	North Yorkshire
Cleveland	Lancashire	Nottinghamshire
Cumbria	Leicestershire	Shropshire
Derbyshire	Lincolnshire	Staffordshire
Durham	Northumberland	

GROUP B

Those within the areas of the following non-metropolitan counties—

Avon	Essex	Northamptonshire
Bedfordshire	Gloucestershire	Oxfordshire
Berkshire	Hampshire	Somerset
Buckinghamshire	Hereford and Worcester	Suffolk
Cambridgeshire	Hertfordshire	Surrey
Cornwall	The Isle of Wight	Warwickshire
Devon	The Isles of Scilly	West Sussex
Dorset	Kent	Wiltshire
East Sussex	Norfolk	

GROUP C

Those within the areas of the metropolitan districts of England.

GROUP D

Those within the area of Greater London.

GROUP E

Those in Wales.

GROUP F

Those in Scotland.

GROUP G

Those in Northern Ireland.

Articles 45 and 52   SCHEDULE 3

TRANSITORY PROVISIONS

PART I

ESTABLISHMENT OF INITIAL SAMPLE

1. For the purpose of establishing the initial sampling points, Article 38 shall have effect subject to the following modifications.

2. Paragraph (1) shall have effect as if there were substituted the following provision:—

"(1) The Registrar shall, not later than three months after the coming into operation of Part IV, designate in accordance with paragraph (6) those service points which are to serve as the initial sampling points".

3. If notices given under Article 38(6)(a) specify periods beginning after the first day of the first sampling year—

(a) paragraph (2)(c) shall have effect as if the reference to the beginning of each sampling year were a reference to the beginning of the third and each subsequent sampling year, and

(b) for the purposes of paragraph (2)(d) the period before the beginning of the second sampling year shall be disregarded.

PART II

INITIAL PAYMENT TO AUTHORS

1. If notices given under Article 38(6)(a) specify periods beginning after the first day of the first sampling year then, for the purpose of ascertaining, in the

financial year in which the first sampling year ends, sums due by way of Public Lending Right, Articles 42 and 46 shall have effect subject to the following modifications.

2. Articles 42(2) and 46(4) shall have effect as if any reference to the sampling year were a reference to so much thereof as falls on and after the day from which loans are required to be recorded.

Article 49   **SCHEDULE 4**

PAYMENT MANDATE

"Please forward, until further notice, all sums that may from time to time become due to me/us or the survivor(s) of us by way of Public Lending Right to *[here state full name and address of the bank, firm or person to whom payments are to be sent]* or *[where payment is to be made to a Bank]* to such other Branch of that Bank as the Bank may from time to time request. Your compliance with this request shall discharge the Registrar's liability in respect of such sums."

Date ....   Signature ....

                                        Name ....
                                        (Block Capitals)

                                        Address ....

                                        ....

                                        ....

EXPLANATORY NOTE
(This Note is not part of the Order.)

This Order brings into force the Public Lending Right Scheme 1982, under which authors are enabled to receive annual payments in respect of loans of their books from public libraries.

Parts I, II and IV, which are brought into force on 14th June 1982, define the scope of the Scheme and provide for the recording of loans at a number of designated libraries.

Part III, brought into force on 1st September 1982, sets out the arrangements for authors to register books which are eligible under the Scheme, and to transfer or renounce an interest in any particular book.

Part V, brought into force on 1st July 1983, provides for authors to receive payments under the Scheme, at a rate of 0.5p for each loan.

1983 No. 480

LIBRARIES

The Public Lending Right Scheme 1982 (Amendment) Order 1983

Made - - - - -	25th March 1983
Laid before Parliament	8th April 1983
Coming into Operation	1st May 1983

The Secretary of State for Education and Science, in exercise of the powers conferred by section 3(7) of the Public Lending Right Act 1979(a) and after consulting with representatives of authors and library authorities and of others who appear likely to be affected, hereby makes the following Order:—

1. This Order may be cited as the Public Lending Right Scheme 1982 (Amendment) Order 1983 and shall come into operation on 1st May 1983.

2.—(1) In paragraph (2) of Article 6 of the Public Lending Right Scheme 1982(b) (eligible books)—

(a) the words "of printed text" shall be omitted;

(b) the words after "four or more authors" shall be omitted from sub-paragraph (b) of the proviso; and

(c) the following provision shall be inserted after the said sub-paragraph (b):—
"(bb) a book which is wholly or mainly a musical score;".

(2) The following provision shall be substituted for paragraph (3) of the said Article 6:—

"(3) The pages referred to in paragraph (2) are pages, including end-papers, other than blank pages".

Keith Joseph,
Secretary of State for
Education and Science.

25th March 1983.

(a) 1979 c. 10.   (b) The Scheme is set out in the Appendix to S.I. 1982/719.

EXPLANATORY NOTE

(This Note is not part of the Order.)

This Order amends provisions of the Public Lending Right Scheme 1982 which define the books which may be registered under the Scheme. The provisions specifying the minimum number of pages of an eligible book are modified so as to allow all pages other than blank pages to be taken into account, rather than only pages of printed text as hitherto. The restriction relating to books with more than one author is relaxed so as to make encyclopaedias, dictionaries and comparable publications with two or three authors eligible for registration. Musical scores are specifically excluded.

Index